My Story, Inkeri's Journey

Essays and poetry by
Inkeri Väänänen-Jensen

Penfield
Press

ACKNOWLEDGMENTS

I wish to acknowledge the support and encouragement of Hannele Jönsson and Dr. K. Börje Vähämäki, both from Finland, in whose classes in the Department of Scandinavian Studies at the University of Minnesota I began my work of reading Finnish and translating from Finnish to English.

I wish to thank Tuulikki Sinks, also of the Department of Scandinavian Studies at the University of Minnesota, for her support, her encouragement, and her willingness to read my work. "Kiitos" to all three of these fine teachers!

This is one small part of a Minnesota Finnish-American history project begun in 1979 by the Minnesota Finnish-American Historical Society, aided by a grant and other support from the Minnesota Historical Society, and spearheaded by three people of Finnish descent—Velma Doby, an immigration specialist, Jeanne Maki, a lawyer, and Carl Ross, a labor historian. More than a hundred family histories and over two-hundred hours of oral tapes from this project are available for study at the Immigration History Research Center in St. Paul, Minnesota.

I wish to thank my husband, Harald Jensen, for his encouragement, general support, and proofreading help during the long time it took to bring this book to fruition.

Note: Although my "American" name is Ingrid Jensen, I use my Finnish maiden name, Inkeri Väänänen, with my married last name, Jensen, whenever I work with Finnish-related material.

—*Inkeri Väänänen-Jensen*

Editors: Joanne Asala, Miriam Canter, Dorothy Crum, Georgia Heald, Joan Liffring-Zug, John Zug. Graphic Artist: Robyn Loughran.

Books by Mail: Postpaid to one address. Prices subject to change.
This book: $13.00

Titles translated by Inkeri Väänänen-Jensen:
Finnish Short Stories. $14.95   *Forbidden Fruit and Other Tales*
The Fish of Gold and Other   *by Juhani Aho.* $14.95
    Finnish Folk Tales. $9.95
Finnish Proverbs. $8.95
Other titles of Finnish interest:
Fantastically Finnish: Recipes and Traditions
    Recipes edited by Beatrice Ojakangas.$8.95
Fine Finnish Foods
    By Gerry Kangas and others.$6.95   Catalog of all titles: $2.00
The Best of Finnish Americana: 1978-1994   Penfield Press
    Edited by Michael G. Karni and   215 Brown Street
    Joanne Asala. $16.95   Iowa City, Iowa 52245-5842

Dedicated to the Memory
of Otto and Lempi Väänänen
Immigrants from Finland

Foreword

This book is about growing up as a "Finn kid" in America or, more
specifically, the Iron Range towns of Ely and Virginia in northern
Minnesota in the 1920s and 1930s. It is also about adult life—how
being the child of immigrant parents influenced that life, and still
influences it today. Other Finnish immigrant children might tell a
different story, but this book represents Finnish immigrant life as
I saw it. I have tried to write as honestly as I could. No attempt has
been made to fictionalize either the people or the events.

—*Inkeri Väänänen-Jensen (1994)*

ontents

My Father, an Immigrant

Otto Vilhelm Väänänen

Otto had been,
Since the time of his youth,
A subject of the Russian Czar,
Nicholas the Second, Emperor of all the Russias.
He was also the son
Of an enterprising farmer,
Who had developed
Five farms for his five sons.
But Czar Nicholas had other plans
For Finland's young men.
He simply dissolved
The whole Finnish army
And conscripted them
For Russia's Imperial Army,
To serve anywhere in the world.
Leaving his inheritance behind him,
Young Otto borrowed his brother's passport
And sailed away to a New World.

My Mother, an Immigrant

Lempi Katri Helander-Väänänen

Famine and poverty were daily companions
In the two-room log cottage
Her family of six called home.
They ate the inner bark of the pine tree
As part of the flour in their bread.
Four of the family's eight children
Died in their early infancy,
Too frail to win the struggle for life.
Her mother's early death,
And a strange, new stepmother
Sent her from home at fourteen
To clean and cook in someone else's house,
The only work she felt she knew how to do.
At eighteen, she left for the nearby city
And became a spinner in a textile mill.
After eight years of this factory work,
She heeded adventure's timely call,
And in 1911 she sailed to America,
To open that golden door to a golden land.

*Mrs. Heleni (left) sent Lempi Helander
her ticket from Finland to America.*

*In Finland, prior to emigration, Lempi Helander (far right) is shown
visiting her childhood home and father Mikko (left) with his second wife
and their children, Elli and Martti.*

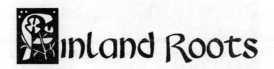

inland Roots

In the early 1900s two Finns, a young man, Otto Väänänen, and a young woman, Lempi Helander, arrived in the United States on different ships. They met in Minnesota, were married, and lived their lives among Finnish and other immigrants on Minnesota's Iron Range, in the cities of Ely and Virginia.

Who were they, these two immigrants, my parents? Why did they come here? What did they find?

Written records of my father's family exist only from 1705, the year when the Nilsiä church in Finland burned and all the church records were destroyed. But words-of-mouth do exist back to 1556 when the Swedish government, then the government of Finland, rewarded three Finnish soldier comrades for their bravery by giving each of them 3,000 hectares, about 7,500 acres, of land. One of these soldiers was a Väänänen and his gift of land lay on the shores of the great Kallavesi Lake, near the city of Kuopio. This land became the village of Väänälän Ranta, or Väänänen's Shore. About 100 years later, in the 1660s, some of the Väänänens moved north and east to the parish of Nilsiä, into the tiny village of Reittiö. Much later, as a young man, my grandfather, Heikki (Henry) Väänänen, a well-to-do farmer, moved a few miles to the north into the village of Jumiskylä (the village of a mythical being) in the parish of Varpaisjärvi (Lake of Saplings), which is in Eastern Finland in the province of Savo, the principal city of which is Kuopio. And it is here that I begin my story.

My Father

My father, Otto Vilhelm Väänänen, was born October 13, 1883, the son of Heikki Väänänen and his second wife, Johanna Maria Huttunen (1854-1929), who lived on a farm called Rosinmäki, originally Rosilanmäki. The meaning of the farm name has been lost through the years, but it has been conjectured that at one time it could have meant hill of horses, *maki* being hill.

During his lifetime Grandfather Heikki eventually owned five farms with a total area of 1,600 hectares, about 4,000 acres, most of it in forest. To accumulate this land, in addition to farming, which brought in practically no cash income, Heikki worked as an entrepreneur, going by boat along the lakes and canals of eastern Finland into the city of St. Petersburg, the capital of Russia (from 1717 to 1917), to bring back goods to sell: coffee, salt, spices, and cloth. During the winter months, he and his neighbors drove their large sleighs over the frozen ground hauling tar to St. Petersburg and bringing back goods to sell. In good traveling weather, they could cover 100 kilometers in a day, a tremendous feat. At this time Finland was a Russian grand duchy, so St. Petersburg served as Finland's capital, too.

Heikki was married twice and fathered fourteen children, each wife bearing seven. He married Anna Liisa Rissanen (1838-1873) on August 18, 1862, when he was twenty-six and she was twenty-four. They had five girls and two boys, all born in the 1860s and 1870s—years of famine in Finland.

When Anna Liisa died at thirty-five, the oldest of her surviving children was ten. Two children died during their first year of life, and the other five all died of tuberculosis. Only the youngest, Maria Karoliina, lived past forty, and she died at forty-two.

In June, 1875, Heikki married Johanna Huttunen, my grandmother. She was twenty-one; he was thirty-nine. They had five sons and two daughters, including Otto, my father (1883-1949), and Lassi, who was only forty-four when he died in 1919—of tuberculosis! By now this was called the family disease. Each of the five sons, my father included, was to receive one of the five farms. When the two daughters, Miina and Hilma, married, they took with them, as was the custom, only *myyniä* (a dowry) of bed and kitchen linens, quilts, towels, rugs, scarves, blouses, and skirts—whatever may have been accumulated as a hope chest.

During my childhood I met two descendants from the first seven children, Joopi (Josef) Väänänen and Emil Väänänen. Joopi stayed with us in Ely during the early 1920s, and returned to Finland. Emil came to Ely, and married Senja Teppo of Florenton, a rural Finnish community near Virginia. They moved to Waukegan, Illinois, where he worked as a carpenter. In 1934 Emil moved back to Finland with his wife and two children, Helen and Vernon. It is my understanding that he had originally entered the United States illegally. In 1940 the two children returned to the United States, going to their mother's

12

relatives in Chicago. At that time Finland was engaged in the bitter Winter War with Russia, and since Helen and Vernon were American citizens, the family decided they would be safer in the United States. Also, Vernon preferred to serve in the United States military rather than in the Finnish army. In World War II, Vernon was on a ship torpedoed in the Indian Ocean, and in 1944 he took part in the Allied invasion of Normandy. Helen worked in Chicago. She was an attractive, high-spirited, quick-to-laugh, happy young woman. In 1944 we were shocked to learn that at age twenty-four, Helen died suddenly of tuberculosis. At that time, the illness from which she died was called "galloping consumption."

Growing up on the Rosinmäki farm with his four brothers and two sisters, and planning to become a farmer himself, my father, Otto, helped with the farm work and learned fishing skills on the nearby lakes and rivers. There were always hired men working on the large farm lands that his father Heikki was developing for his sons, and Otto often remarked to us later that there were never less than fifteen at the table for each meal. I have a vague recollection that each one had his own wooden spoon and that eating was from a common bowl or bowls.

In the Varpaisjärvi parish, children were taught to read and write by a teacher who traveled from farm to farm holding classes. From time to time, the large Rosinmäki farmhouse was the center for the learning classes, which usually lasted four weeks and to which children from neighboring farms came to learn to read and write. Children of many different ages were grouped into the one class. One of these four-week sessions, as far as I have been able to learn, was the only classroom type of education Otto had. Also, it is a sad commentary that the preceding few sentences cover *all* I know about my father's early life in Finland. However, Uncle Paavo was in his teens when his brother, my father, left for America, and he remembered Otto with warmth during all his life—Otto, who was forever remembered in his childhood home and rural neighborhood as a light-hearted, merry young fellow.

From about 1155, Finland was an integral part of Sweden, but in 1809, as part of the Napoleonic wars, the country was wrested from Swedish control by the Russians. In the beginning, Finland had considerable autonomous power, including a number of constitutional rights. Independence would not come until 1917.

Czar Nicholas II had sworn an oath to protect Finland's special autonomous status, but in 1894 he began to withdraw many of the constitutional rights, and Russification of Finland began in earnest, including censorship of the press, dismissal and also imprisonment of civil servants, abolition of the Finnish postal system, forced teaching and use of the Russian language, and the granting by the Czar of dictatorial powers to the Russian governor-general of Finland, which included the power of banishment. A ban on freedom of speech, association, and assembly was imposed. The governor-general received unlimited authority to destroy Finland's status as an autonomous grand duchy. In 1901 Czar Nicholas II ordered the Finnish army dissolved, with Finnish soldiers to become a part of the Russian army to serve anywhere in the Russian empire. More than fifty percent of the conscripts failed to appear for the first registration in the spring of 1902. In the area around the village of Isokyrö in western Finland, ninety young men were called for military service in 1902, but only nineteen reported at the induction center. The others had fled to America.

Fearing induction into the hated Russian Imperial Army and observing with dread the spread of autocratic rule, my father, Otto Vilhelm, heir to one of the family's five farms, decided to flee. The Varpaisjärvi parish records state that on December 29, 1902, he applied for permission from the State Church to leave the country. No one could get a legal passport without a certificate of character from the parish church. A 1920 application for an American passport for a visit back to Finland states that he had gone to the city of Hanko on the southeastern shore of Finland, Hanko being the chief embarking place for emigrating Finns. Here his suitcase, with his passport, was stolen, but he did leave Hanko by ship for Liverpool, England. In our childhood, a rumor circulated that he finally used a cousin's passport. However, I have learned that my father used his brother Heikki Juho's passport to get to America. Because of his very flat feet, Heikki Juho did not pass the army physical exam and so did not need to flee to America. Dr. William Hoglund, a Finnish scholar, states that some Finns arrived in America without passports. Also, newly arrived immigrants sent their passports back home to be used by a friend or relative. My father arrived with a "borrowed" passport, his brother's.

Otto's naturalization papers indicate that he sailed to Quebec, Canada, and from there took the Canadian Pacific Railroad to Port Arthur (today's Thunder Bay). From there he sailed on the S.S.

America, arriving in Duluth July 15, 1905.

For the next three years Otto worked as an iron ore miner in Mt. Iron, and for two and a half years he worked in Biwabik and Aurora as a machine operator *(koneenkäytäjä)* in a mine. He then moved to Ely, where he was also employed in the iron mines. The names, Zenith and Pioneer, remain in my memory from childhood.

After several years of less than satisfactory conscriptions, the Russian government abandoned the attempt to force the Finns to serve in the Imperial Army. Young Finnish men were saved from being sent to fight in the 1905 Russo-Japanese War. Finns were released from personal military service and Finland had to pay a small annual tax to the Russian treasury as compensation.

My Mother

My mother, Lempi Katri Helander, was born August 14, 1885, in southeastern Finland in Kauppilankylä, which is the general term used to denote a small country village. It actually means "the village where the store is." This village was in the Eräjärvi (Lake in the Wilderness) parish, in the province of Häme. She was the daughter and granddaughter of country tailors. Her grandfather was Henrik Karlsson Helander (1830-1910). Her grandmother was Fredrika Kaarlentytär, or "Karl's Daughter" (1827-1868). The Eräjärvi church records list no last name for the grandmother. She is simply "Karl's Daughter," which is the patronymic name form derived from her father's first name.

Lempi's father, Mikko Maurits Helander (1856-1921), was Henrik and Fredrika's only surviving child. Three sons and a daughter died in childhood or in early youth. Three years after his first wife's death, Lempi's grandfather Henrik married Maijastiina Wallenius (1822-1907) from the nearby town of Orivesi. She was forty-eight, he was forty-one. There were no children from this marriage.

Mikko Helander married Maria Kaarlentytär (Karl's Daughter) Metsä (Woods or Forest) from the nearby parish of Längelmäki, where she was born in 1853. Mikko Helander and Maria Metsä had eight children, four of whom died within a few weeks after birth and four of whom survived to adulthood. The surviving children were Thekla Tyyne, 1881; Martta Siviä, 1883; Lempi Katri (my mother), 1885, and Uuno Julius, 1889.

During my childhood, my mother rarely spoke about happy times during her childhood. Most frequently she spoke of the times of hunger, poverty, and fear, which, as a child, I could never really understand, or even appreciate. In fact, I didn't even want to listen. She bore major wounds from her childhood; hearing about them made me uneasy, impatient. I didn't want to hear about them, for there was nothing I could do to change them or to assuage their pain.

Eventually, I learned that Finland has had a long history of wars and famines. From the early 1300s until 1809 Finland, as a part of Sweden, was involved in a long series of wars between Sweden and Russia—wars fought for the most part on Finnish soil, wars in which soldiers and noncombatants alike were killed, the land ravaged. By 1695 the population of Finland had risen to around 500,000; by 1730 it was about 200,000. Thousands of soldiers had been killed; early frosts ruined crops, causing famine; thousands of Finns had been taken as captives into Russia; epidemics had raged throughout the land. Finland has suffered a series of famines that caused many deaths, including those of the late 1860s, 1892 to 1894, and 1903.

In 1892 my mother was seven years old, old enough to remember the hardships of that and the following years. In their simple, two-room log house they ground the inner white bark of pine trees as part of the flour for their bread. She also remembered the infant deaths, the three baby sisters who died in 1892, 1894, and in 1897. As an adult in America, Lempi still recoiled from the memory of these deaths. The three who had died in the depths of winter were placed in the family *aitta,* a storage shed built in 1775, until the ground would thaw enough for burial.

All of the Helander children attended the public elementary school *(kansakoulu)* in the parish of Eräjärvi. Lempi entered the school in September, 1895, when she was ten years old. She received her certificate of completion, or graduation *(Päästötodistus),* on June 3, 1899, after four years of schooling. This was the total amount of formal schooling that she, the daughter of a humble cottager, received in Finland.

Sometime in the seventeenth century, the ability to read and write had become a condition for the exercise of civil rights in Finland. For instance, a Finn could not be confirmed or marry without knowing how to read and write. In most parishes the Finnish minister had the responsibility of teaching reading and writing to prepare the Finnish-speaking youths for religious confirmation in Finnish, and also to "qualify" them for marriage. Aleksis Kivi in his 1870 Finnish novel, *Seitsemän veljestä* (The Seven Brothers), gives a humorous description of a minister's travail in teaching reading to seven brothers ranging in age from eighteen to twenty-five. For many in the rural parishes, this was the only formal-type schooling they received. Not until 1922 would an elementary school education be made compulsory. Until 1848 schools in Finland were conducted in Swedish. Swedish had been the official language of Finland for many years. In 1848, the first elementary school in the Finnish language was established, and not until ten years later, in 1858, was a Finnish section introduced into the Swedish secondary school in the city of Jyväskylä.

As a tailor, Lempi's grandfather had done all his stitching by hand. When Lempi's father purchased a simple pedal sewing machine, her grandfather could never accept it and refused to use it—the machine was too modern and could not be trusted to do good work. Lempi learned the tailoring trade as a young girl, helping her father and grandfather in their work, helping them to sew men's coats and trousers.

On February 1, 1899, at the age of forty-six, Lempi's mother, Maria Metsä, died from a chronic kidney inflammation (*munuais tauti*). After her mother's death in February, Lempi finished school in June. Now fourteen, she left home to serve as a housemaid for a woman schoolteacher. Lempi remembered her as a very demanding and cranky woman. It was not a happy experience. In November of 1899, Lempi's father married Elsa Edvardintytär (Edward's Daughter) Salminen (1873-1957) from the parish of Längelmäki, which had also been the home of Lempi's mother. Elsa was twenty-six and Lempi's father was forty-three. Lempi resented that her father had married so soon after the death of her mother, and she rarely came home. After reading two letters written to Lempi after her arrival in America, I could sense discord in the relationship between Lempi and her father and Elsa. Four children were born during this second marriage, with two girls dying in infancy. The two surviving children were Elli Mariaana (1905-1971) and Martti Viljo (1909-1977). Years later I somehow sensed that Lempi was ashamed that her father was still fathering children. Lempi was twenty-four and her oldest sister was twenty-nine when little Martti was born; their father was fifty-three. To Lempi that was too old to be having babies. I have an old battered picture in which Lempi poses with her father, her stepmother Elsa, and their two children, Elli, who looks to be about four or five years old, and Martti, still a baby. It was Lempi's farewell visit to her childhood home.

Around 1900, industry began to accelerate in Finland and the children of the humble cottagers in the Finnish countryside thronged into the towns and cities. The Helander children followed this national trend. In 1903, at the age of eighteen, Lempi moved to the city of Tampere, where her sister Martta lived. The Eräjärvi church records show that the four surviving children in the family all left home permanently around the age of eighteen. The oldest, Thekla Tyyne, went to the nearby town of Orivesi, the other three farther away to the larger Tampere. In Tampere Lempi got work in a Swedish textile factory, *Tammerfors Klädesfabriks Aktie-Bolag* (Tampere Clothes Manufacturing, Ltd.), where she worked four years in the spinning section while living at a boardinghouse for textile factory workers.

By now, both of her sisters were living in Tampere so Lempi once again had a social life within her family. In addition, she became good friends with a young girl, Mari Maenpää, who served as the seamstress and maid-of-all-work in the boardinghouse owned and operated by Rouva (Mrs.) Heleni. For some reason, in 1907 Lempi asked for her release from the factory. I have the original copy of her release and reference paper dated October 11, 1907, signed by August Lundholm and stating that she had been a good worker. She and Mari now moved to work in the city of Pietarsaari (Peter's Island), a coastal town considerably north and west of Tampere. They stayed there for three years, working in a textile factory. Mrs. Heleni, the owner of the Tampere boardinghouse, had gone to America and some years later, in 1910, she sent tickets to Lempi and Mari for passage to Ely, Minnesota, where Mrs. Heleni now lived. Since Mrs. Heleni had sent her the America ticket, and she also had a good friend to travel with, Lempi may have made the decision to leave Finland without too much difficulty, particularly since her Eräjävi home no longer seemed a comfortable place for her even to visit. Also, she may have felt that her work in Swedish-owned textile factories promised little opportunity for advancement, especially since she was not Swedish-speaking. Mrs. Heleni must have convinced her that better opportunities awaited her in America. Once in America, Lempi worked as a housemaid in the home of a mining *kapteeni* (captain) in a place she always referred to as Åtrikki, an early Iron Range mining town that no longer exists. I have since discovered that the American name of the town was Adriatic, a name unpronounceable to a recently arrived immigrant Finn: "Åtrikki" was as close as Lempi could come.

In Ely she met a young miner, Otto Väänänen, and they were married in Ely, November 26, 1912, with two Finnish friends, Matti Kuitunen and Minnie Viljamaa, as witnesses. Otto was twenty-nine years old, Lempi twenty-seven. According to a clipping in the Ely newspaper, Otto was a "mining captain" at the Lucky Boy property. Captain *(kapteeni),* a nautical term brought over by Cornish miners, was the name used for supervisors in the mines.

Lempi and her brother Uuno were the only members of the Helander family to immigrate to America, Uuno in 1910, Lempi in 1911. She remembered that Uuno's friends gave him a gala farewell at the train station in Tampere. They expected great things of this handsome young man (he was twenty-one) as he left on his American adventure.

Mari Maenpää, Lempi's friend who was now called the American "Mary," worked as a housemaid for a Finnish family in Ely, the Palmgards, whose name, in my memory at least, was pronounced Pankooli in Finnish. Later Mary worked as a waitress at Ronka's, a Finnish restaurant in Ely. In 1918, she married Antti (Andrew) Kivipelto (Rockfield).

Soon after Lempi's and Mari's arrival in Ely, Mrs. Heleni and her husband, Matti, moved to a farm in Embarrass, Minnesota (called *Imperia* by the Finns). In later years we often visited the Heleni farm in *Imperia,* where their large, unpainted, log house weathered to a silver gray through the years. I remember that we children were bored visiting the Heleni farm, where the adults just talked and talked and laughed and laughed, drank coffee, and ate. Of course, we got something to eat, too. But as city children we had not developed an interest in cows or in pigs. The stench from the pigsty violated our tender nostrils, and we held our noses against it. Also, the flies in the barnyard, and even in the house, bothered us. The only English reading material in the house was the Sears Roebuck catalog and after several visits, we found that catalog boring. We had not yet thought to bring our own reading material when we went on trips.

Lempi Katri Helander came to America to seek a life better than the one she had known. She was twenty-five years old and willing to take a chance on "a new life." Perhaps it was not so much what the

19

future in America might hold in store for her that influenced her decision, but rather the desire to leave behind her a life of limited opportunity and of strained family relationships. On her passport, written in Russian and dated December 22, 1910, she indicated that she intended to stay in the United States five years. She stayed for sixty-five years, until her death. As I write this story, I am wondering whether in later years she, as one of the millions who passed through Ellis Island, considered that Island truly her "golden door" to a "golden land."

hildhood in Ely, Minnesota

After their marriage on November 26, 1912, Otto and Lempi Väänänen settled in Ely, where they had both been working, she as a housemaid, he as a miner. They rented a small white house on West Harvey Street while building their own little house across the street. By 1919, four children had been born: Irma Helena in 1914; I, Inkeri Eleanoora in 1915; a brother, Jorma Vilhelm in 1917; and Irene Elisabet in 1919.

On July 22, 1916, Otto signed a Declaration of Intention to become a citizen of the United States: "It is my bona fide intention to renounce forever all allegiance and fidelity to any foreign prince, potentate, state, or sovereignty, and particularly to Nicholas II, Emperor of All the Russias, of whom I am now a subject....I am not an anarchist; I am not a polygamist nor a believer in the practice of polygamy; and it is my intention in good faith to become a citizen of the United States of America and to permanently reside therein: SO HELP ME GOD."

On July 23, 1918, he signed a Petition for Naturalization, which two Finnish friends from Ely, Jacob Riikola and Andrew Luhtanen, signed as witnesses. On November 16, 1918, after signing an oath of allegiance, also witnessed by two Ely Finnish friends, Gust Maki and John Palmgard, Otto became an American citizen and was issued Certificate of Naturalization Number 873909.

When Otto became a citizen, Lempi, according to existing law, also assumed citizenship without going to citizenship classes or passing any special tests. From 1855 until 1922, the wife, and children under the age of sixteen, became citizens when the husband and father became a naturalized citizen. For those born in the United States, citizenship was automatic.

My earliest memories are of living in a small white bungalow on West Harvey Street. Our father, with the help of friends, had dug out a part of the cellar and had also helped to build the house, working in the evenings and on Sundays. It had a large kitchen, a dining room, one bedroom, a bathroom, a front room, and a small unfinished attic. The living room was always called the front room, called either a *frontti ruuma* or *rontti ruuma*, depending on what part of Finland your parents were from. The kitchen opened into a dining room, which in turn had a door leading to a food pantry with open shelves on three walls. The floor of this pantry was in large part a trap door which, when pulled up by its sunken iron ring, opened to the partially dug earth cellar where apples, oranges, and root vegetables were stored. I loved the smell of that cellar when potatoes were stored there. The bathroom off the kitchen held only a toilet, but there was enough room for a lavatory sink and a bathtub—future refinements to be added when the money was available. For the present, it was enough for the family to walk every Saturday to take a *sauna* (a Finnish steam bath) at Ahola's Public Bathhouse three blocks away. There the whole family bathed together, enjoying the *löyly* (steam), slapping ourselves vigorously with *vihtas* (switches) made of birch boughs and leaves, washing, and splashing out of pails of warm water. It never entered our minds that it might be considered odd for the whole family to bathe together. Both of my parents had grown up with the *sauna* as a part of their heritage, for *saunas* had existed in Finland for some two-thousand years. In the rural homes of Finland the *sauna,* or bathhouse, was a separate building, usually built of logs, and if at all possible, beside a lake, a stream, or the sea. Most of the time "taking a *sauna"* was a group affair within the family.

In the only bedroom in the house, our mother and father slept in a double bed, little Irene Elizabet in a crib a few feet across from their bed. Jorma slept on padding and blankets on the floor, his head and shoulders in the one clothes closet, the rest of him extended into the bedroom. Irma and I slept in the front room on the *lounssi* (lounge), which had a wooden frame, a leather seat and back, arms of wood, and opened into a double bed. Once in a while Irma and I slept on the floor of the small, unfinished attic.

In our front room we had a large, spreading fern growing out of a large yellow-and-green bowl set on a high, wooden plant stand. It seemed that every Finnish home we visited in Ely had a big fern in the *rontti ruuma*. We also had a large cat which persisted in leaping up into the flowerpot and wetting the soil around the fern. I think I remember the fern so well because of the excitement of shooing the cat off the fern. He leaped off with such grace and speed even though we shooed him off unceremoniously.

Many Finnish homes we visited had a standard piece of equipment, usually placed in the front room where visitors congregated. It was called a spittoon, a floor receptacle made of brass or enamel. I am almost ashamed to write about these spittoons, for their use seems so crude now in retrospect. It was, however, a frequently used item, particularly when there was company. In the 1920s many men smoked cigarettes or cigars, or chewed snuff, and a spittoon was considered a necessary receptacle. It was something we children abhorred, although we never said anything about our feelings. Later, a more elegant-sounding word, "cuspidor," replaced "spittoon," but use of the "cuspidor" remained an ugly custom to us.

We had a large back yard, most of which was in garden with vegetables and flowers, but mostly vegetables, particularly root crops: potatoes, carrots, and beets, plus cucumbers, beans, and cabbages. These were the familiar vegetables from Finland. Rhubarb plants (pieplants) were also plentiful—providing sauces and fluffy pink puddings for desserts. An unpainted gray coal shack stood in one corner of the back yard, next to the alley. We washed it up for a playhouse during the summers; it was about four feet square, eight feet high.

Our family's closest friends were, of course, other Finns, particularly the Antti Kivipelto family. Mrs. Kivipelto was Mary (Mari) Maenpää, Lempi's friend from the boardinghouse days in Finland and her companion on the trip to America. The two women remained close friends until my mother's death in 1975 at the age of eighty-nine. Mary died two years later; she was eighty-seven.

Antti Kivipelto spoke English better than most Finnish men we knew, having served in the United States Army during World War I. He was a kind, gentle man—tall, slender, and handsome. After working for a while in the iron ore mines in Ely, which he disliked, he worked as a janitor in the Ely Memorial High School, and to us children of Finnish miners, he had truly risen on the employment ladder. We were proud when we heard that some "American" at the school had called Antti a "real gentleman." The Kivipeltos had five children: two boys, Oiva (meaning splendid, superb, first-rate) and Aimo (good, sound, brave), and three girls, Irma, Evelyn, and Ruutti (Ruth). We were all good friends for many years. When Antti died unexpectedly in 1946 at the age of fifty-six, it was a shock and a great loss to our whole family. Other family friends included the Mäenpää family: the father, Fapiaani (Fabian), the mother, Mary (nee Perkiö), and the children, Vieno (mild, gentle), Viivi (Vivian), Vilho, and Venni. They operated a dairy farm in White Iron, a rural community near Ely. In my recollection, they were the only successful Finnish farmers we knew while we lived in Ely. Most other Finnish farmers of our acquaintance, including Fapiaani's brother Jussi (John), were barely scratching out a living on their small, rocky, unproductive farms. As I remember, the mother, Mary, provided the spark and energy for the Mäenpääs' successful farming enterprise. They had a lovely large house at the top of a hill, a big barn, a fine sauna. A river meandered through their land below the hill, and it was on that winding river that I learned to row a boat. Since Mäenpää means "hilltop" and the farmhouse was on top of a hill, the Mäenpää farm was fittingly known as the Hillcrest Dairy Farm. We thought it a "high-toned" name for a Finnish farm and that the name somehow made the Mäenpääs a *real* part of the American scene, something we did not feel about ourselves. For many years the Mäenpääs delivered fresh raw milk to our house and to many others in Ely. Those were the days before the law required pasteurizing of milk. Sometimes during the summers, Irma and I stayed with the Mäenpääs and

Posing on the old truck
at Hillcrest Dairy Farm, White Iron, Minnesota.

helped with the washing and sterilizing of the milk bottles. Cleaning and washing the milk separator daily was, as I recall, a real chore usually left to Mrs. Mäenpää, who possessed boundless energy and good will. Fapiaani also butchered, and with a horse and wagon delivered fresh meat to Ely families. In the Mäenpääs' outhouse we were introduced to the use of the Sears Roebuck catalog. We soon learned to skip the shiny, colored pages.

We loved rowing along the river, which led to One Pine Lake, where we swam along its rocky shores.

The John E. Porthan (or *Porttaani* as we pronounced it) family lived in a large stucco house across the street from us. Laura, the youngest of their twelve children, whose twin sister Martha had died in infancy, was our best friend. Mr. Porthan managed the general merchandise store, the Finnish Stock Company. He spoke English well, and for a time was the mayor of Ely. We were proud to know him as somehow we felt he was one Finn who had "made it" on the American scene. He was the only Finn I knew who did not drink coffee. At our house his cup was always filled with hot water to which he added sugar and cream. Mrs. Porthan had died in 1917 at the age of forty-three, and for some time the family had a good-natured housekeeper, Mrs. Laitinen. Mr. Porthan later remarried, and our relationship with the family was never the same again. Henceforth, when we went to get Laura to come out to play, we stood quietly in front of the woodbox beside the kitchen stove until she was ready to come out. Before, we had roamed freely with Laura throughout their marvelous, roomy, three-story house. We especially admired the heavy wooden sliding doors that closed off the front room from the downstairs hall. From time to time Laura slid the doors back and forth for our benefit. We were also impressed by the fact that her father had a study across the hall.

Since Laura's father was the manager of the Finnish Stock Company, Laura had a "proprietary" feeling toward the store. Irma and I would often go with her to one of the grocery clerks and ask for broken cookies and rotten bananas. Occasionally we got some, but not always. All the clerks in the store were Finnish. We would also go down into the basement to the toilet, and to pick up cardboard boxes which we carried to the nearby bakery and sold for a few pennies apiece. Our family never entered the door of the bakery to buy bread or rolls, or other bakery products. No self-respecting Finnish housewife, at least none that we knew, would buy "bakery

25

goods." All breads, rolls, and biscuits were made at home. Rings of thick rye hardtack were the only bread we bought in those early years and they came from the Finnish Stock Store. We would use the money from the boxes to go to the silent movies at the Ely Theater. A ticket cost ten cents for those under twelve. Sometimes we begged the cashier to let us in for a nickel apiece, but she never did.

Often in winters Laura wore Indian moccasins—soft, gray, buckskin shoe mocassins. How we envied her and admired her as she walked quietly and effortlessly through the snow while Irma and I clumped along in our four-buckle black "artics."

Laura's brother George had been killed in France in the first World War. George had spent one year at the University of Chicago planning to become a doctor, but volunteered to help "to make the world safe for democracy." His funeral was held in the Washington School auditorium because there was no church in Ely large enough to hold all the people who came to say "farewell." All of this made Laura a special kind of person in our eyes. She was, in truth, our childhood heroine.

Another friend lived across the street in the same yard as the Porthans in a small, white house owned by the Porthans. She came often to visit us during the day, bringing her spinning wheel with her, and we knew her as Perttulan *Mummu* (Grandmother Perttula). We thought *Mummu* was very old. She would spin wool yarn as she and our mother talked and laughed and drank coffee while we children watched and listened. We recognized something noble in Perttulan *Mummu's* personage, and we had the greatest respect for her. I cannot explain what it was. I have since learned that *Mummu's* first name was Eeva and that she had been born on Christmas Eve, 1846, and had come to Ely from Finland in 1893 with her husband and children. After living in Ely for thirty-five years, in the summer of 1928 she moved to Ishpeming, Michigan, to live with her daughter, Miina Perttula-Mäki, a well-known Finnish educator. Not long after, on September 22, 1928, Perttulan *Mummu* died in the home of her daughter. She was then almost eighty-two years of age; she was in her late seventies when we knew her.

Also across the street, next to Perttulan *Mummu,* lived an elderly childless couple, Mr. and Mrs. John Heinonen, who owned a boat and motor. Often during the summers they took our family for rides on the nearby Shawaga Lake, which bordered Ely. We all walked to the lakeshore where the Heinonens kept their boat and motor in one of the many small boathouses that lined the shore on the Ely side of the lake. I can't remember that we children ever thought of misbehaving. We were just happy that the Heinonens cared enough about us to invite us to enjoy rides in their motorboat, something we never expected to own. And we never did.

An Austrian family, the Klobuchars, lived next to the Heinonens. In Ely, Slavic immigrants from central Europe, Slovenians, Croatians, Serbians, Hungarians, and Montenegrins, were all referred to as "Austrians." Until 1918 their countries had all been members of the Austro-Hungarian Empire, and most of them had come to Ely before 1918. Klobuchar's house was set way back on their lot, near the alley, and most of their front land was in vegetable and flower garden. I never knew them very well; they lived so far away. And, of course, they were not Finns.

Our immediate neighbor to the west was an elderly white-haired Austrian woman, Mrs. Iretz, who lived in a small house in the middle of a huge flower and vegetable garden from which she sold both plants and produce. She and my mother often visited over the fence, understanding each other even though they both spoke a broken English, each with her own foreign accent. To us, she was *Airetsin Mummu* (Grandma Iretz).

Next to Mrs. Iretz lived a Finnish family, the Virtanens. They had a large barn, kept cows, and sold milk. They had a daughter, Edna, who had turned deaf in her infancy after a severe illness. As a child, Edna was sent to the School for the Deaf in Faribault, Minnesota, so she eventually became a stranger to us, coming home only occasionally. The Virtanens also had two boys, Aarne and Eino, my brother Jorma's friends. We learned later that Edna died at her school at the age of twelve.

Next to the Virtanens were the Kuukkanens, who had one daughter, Elna. She was older than Irma and I, and once in a while she would come to our house to "play school" with us. She was the teacher, and we prized those times when she, an older girl, condescended to be our teacher. In those days, graduation from the eighth grade was an event; for many immigrant children it was the end of formal schooling. We were given Elna's eighth grade graduation picture. She wore a low-waisted white dress and a large white hair ribbon, and she held a bouquet of flowers in her hands. Elna continued in school, became a teacher in the St. Louis County Schools, and visited our family from time to time through the years, even after we moved from Ely.

Among the Finns, the role of the public school teacher was highly prized. We looked up to teachers, we thought of them as "perfect." Our parents believed that whatever the teacher said or did was right. Many Finnish girls and, a little later, Finnish boys, became teachers, following in the footsteps of the one white collar role model most of us had access to and could reasonably hope to emulate. Young Finns, particularly, among the various Range nationalities, found teaching a way to move up both in the employment and on the social ladders. For the older immigrant children, becoming a teacher was one way out of "menial" work. Being a teacher carried with it a definite prestige, and Finnish parents encouraged their children to go on to college and, if at all possible, gave them financial help. The teachers' colleges in Minnesota in the 1920s and 30s were filled with upwardly mobile immigrant youths, many of them Finnish. Only a few of the first children of the early immigrants studied medicine, law, enginering, theology; most of them became teachers. The general interest and popularity of these other professional fields would come later, would involve younger brothers and sisters, who got help from older brothers and sisters.

We somehow were aware that the public education system formed the backbone of our advance into American society, that somehow education could serve as an equalizing force on the American scene for those of us who had come to look upon ourselves as "unequal" and "inferior."

We believed not only that academic achievement was important but also that it was obtainable. We never questioned our ability to continue our education beyond the high school. We never doubted that we had the "brains" to perform in college. Minnesota's teachers' colleges in Duluth, St. Cloud, Mankato, and Winona, and the University of Minnesota beckoned to many of the immigrant offspring.

But back now to our Ely neighborhood. On the corner, just past the Kuukkanens, lived Tynkelän Anni, or Annabelle Twinkletoes as she was later referred to in English. A small wisp of a gray-haired woman whose thin hair was braided down her back in a sparse pigtail, she lived in a humble, unpainted, silver gray, wooden cottage on the back of her lot, next to the alley. She was an accomplished weaver of rag rugs and one of her small, barren rooms held a large loom. She wove rugs for the Finns, and for others in Ely. We neighborhood children visited her from time to time and she would treat us to Hershey chocolate bars which, as far as I can recollect, she kept under the mattress of her bed. She also treated us to *vanhanpojan käntiä* (bachelor's candies), the flat, round, white pepperment candies marked with x's. A man named Matti lived with her. We understood he was not her husband, just a boarder who worked in the mine.

Next to us on the other, or east side, lived a family named Santapakka (sand mass or hill), who had one son, Yrjö (George). One of Mrs. Santapakka's hands was cut off just above the wrist and she always sore a soft, clean white cloth over it. We accepted her disability and never even thought to ask any questions about it. Years later, when I met their daughter Lillian in West Lafayette, Indiana, where her husband was a professor of mathematics at Purdue University, I learned that their name was now Hill. Lillian was born after we moved from West Harvey Street, so it was a pleasant coincidence to meet her, and we became good friends during the short time we lived in Indiana.

One daily happening involving the Santapakkas stands out clearly in my memory. On the next street, a family named Koski (rapids or falls) kept cows and their grown son Hermanni (Herman) delivered a pail of milk every day to the Santapakkas. Hermanni had an illness which made him lean over backward as he walked. People passing or meeting him on the Ely streets stopped to push him back into an upright position. We always knew when Hermanni was delivering his daily pail of milk to the Santapakkas as, standing on the steps at the back door, he would call out, *"Aukaskaa ovi!"* ("Open the door!"). The door was opened and Hermanni would disappear inside. Later I learned that Hermanni had sleeping sickness and died at the age of twenty-eight.

Although we never did own a boat and motor as the Heinonens did, we did buy a Canadian-made Peterborough canoe, which we kept in a boathouse near Heinonen's boathouse and which we used for trips across Shagawa Lake, portaging to Lillong Lake (Little Long Lake) and to Burntside Lake. I can remember canoeing along a river and meeting Indian families paddling their birchbark canoes. We children, sitting in the bottom of our canoe, only stared in silence and even fear, but Otto would raise his arm and give some kind of greeting. We would stop at an island and camp for several days.It must have been a regular stopping place for campers, as a rough-hewn wooden table and benches were a permanent part of the site. We slept in a tent. Sometimes on these canoe trips, as we paddled across a lake, a storm would rise suddenly. Hurriedly, Father and Mother would paddle to whatever land was closest, beach the canoe, turn it over, and we would all huddle under its protecting umbrella until the storm had passed and we could continue our trip. We children were never afraid of the storms, only excited.

Shagawa Lake bordered Ely and was also known as Long Lake. We neighborhood children walked down to the shore and, wearing white canvas water wings, dog-paddled between the boathouses, splashing about and squealing when small crabs nipped at our toes. Coming out of the water, we fearfully checked our legs and between our toes for bloodsuckers. The word "leech" was not in our vocabulary.

Sometime before 1925, the city of Ely had built a magnificent public beach with many individual dressing rooms and a long boardwalk into the lake. In our swimming suits we sometimes walked along the boardwalk, but usually we just dog-paddled in the water beside it. Going home, we followed the path over a rocky hill where the city water tower loomed into the air and around which gooseberry bushes grew abundantly. We picked and ate the berries, most often when they were still green. I'm not sure we even knew they were not ripe. Sometimes we carried the berries home in our thin, rubber swimming caps and ate them with sugar and cream.

One memory lingers in my mind about being sick in Ely. One day Irma and I were lying in our parents' bed, but I do not recall that we were in any pain. Our mother brought each of us an orange cut in half and sprinkled with sugar, an unusual and wonderful treat. Later we learned that we both had the flu. We were part of the influenza epidemic which raged throughout the world in 1918, killing more than twenty-million people. I was then between three and four years old. Growing up, we discovered that when we had friends who had no living parents, or only one parent, often the missing parents had been victims of that 1918 influenza epidemic.

My name was Inkeri Väänänen, but somehow it was changed to Ingrid Waananen. Whether it happened when I entered school I do not know. It is only recently, since I have become interested in Finnish immigrant life, of which I am a part, that it has even occurred to me to question this early change in my name. Until then I accepted the Americanization of my name without question. How Inkeri became Ingrid, I do not know and it is too late now to find out, for everyone involved in the change has died. As for Väänänen becoming Waananen, I offer this explanation: If *w* does appear in Finnish words it is pronounced as a *v*. Perhaps this helps to explain at least in part how the *V* in Väänänen became written as *W* since *v* and *w* are pronounced the same in Finnish. And, of course, umlauts (¨) disappear in the English language, so the *ä*'s became *a*'s. Hence Väänänen easily became Waananen in America.

The Lincoln Grade School was only a short block from our house and I entered kindergarten there in September, 1920, shortly before my fifth birthday on October 12. I have since learned that the Lincoln School was built in 1908 for $41,000.

I did not know how to speak English and neither did the other children of Finnish, Austrian, Italian, Swedish, Norwegian, and Greek immigrants. I cannot imagine how the kindergarten teacher, whose name is long forgotten, managed a class in which certainly over ninety percent of her pupils did not understand English. The question remains in my mind, "How did she cope?"

From the first grade, one activity stands out in my memory: learning to write my first name that was now Ingrid. The teacher, Helia Koski, herself the child of Finnish immigrants, wrote her pupils' first names on the blackboard with white chalk. Then we each stood at the blackboard tracing our name over and over again until the letters were thick with white chalk and we had each memorized our name's written form. I have wondered how and when we learned to write our last names! I have no recollection of learning to speak English.

From the confines of the third grade room, one event stands out. A boy, not in my room and whose name I can no longer recall, often wet his pants in school. We kids all knew he did this. One day, to our great surprise, his teacher brought him into our room wearing white diapers over his wet pants. She was bringing him to other classrooms also, she said. She must have honestly believed that this kind of treatment would cure him, that shame would cure him. I have wondered if he ever forgot that day. As a mere observer, I have not.

While I was in the third grade, we had another addition to the family, little Theodore. However, he was either born dead or lived only a short while. I never really understood what had happened.

The large schoolyard at Lincoln School had much playground equipment, among which were trapeze rings and horizontal bars.

But I never dared to use these during recess. In those days "bloomer" dresses were in style. A girl's mother would sew a dress, and then make bloomers from the same material. However, for the sake of economy, our mother made the top part of our bloomers from white flour sacks. Under ordinary circumstances, this flour-sack top did not show. Flour was bought in fifty-pound and one-hundred-pound sacks, so white flour-sack material was plentiful. But either our mother did not know about bleaches, or they were not generally available in a small northeastern Minnesota town in the early 1920s, or they were considered an extravagance. Anyhow, sensitive about revealing the lettering on my flour-sack bloomer tops ("Eventually, Why Not Now?," "Pillsbury's Best," "Russell Miller Milling Co."), I never learned to use the trapeze rings or the horizontal bars with the sense of abandon so many girls, who did not have flour-sack bloomers, were able to do. Or at least I used this as an excuse for never becoming adept on the trapeze or the bar.

When it came time for Betty, our youngest, to start kindergarten, which we called "kinigarden," we were so proud of her because she could speak English, something Irma, Jorma, and I had not been able to do when we entered school. We three had trained her for her "kinigarden" debut. That she spoke Finnish clearly and well was not of any value in our eyes. In fact, it was something to be ashamed of. Betty's given name was actually Irene Elisabet. Irene in Finnish is pronounced with three syllables, *I-re-ne*, with the accent on the first syllable and all the vowels "short." But when our mother heard how Irene was pronounced in English—*I-reen* with two vowel sounds, both of them "long"—and with the accent at the end, she immediately switched to the second name, Elisabet, which of course in America became Elizabeth, and eventually the diminutive "Betty."

During the summertime, the janitor at Lincoln School would burn what were considered unneeded school supplies, and then he would carry the ashes just outside the schoolyard fence for pickup by the garbage truck. We sifted through the cooled ashes with the hope of finding something of value—unburned parts of books (we didn't hope for a *whole* book), paper, pens, pencils. But disappointingly, all we ever found were lengths of lead from burned-up pencils.

After I learned to read, I discovered the public library in Ely's Community Center only three short blocks away, and from then on I made regular trips for books. It seemed that most elementary schools had their toilets in the basement, a word that to us became synonymous with "toilet." For years, we called going to the toilet "going to the basement." Later, the first school where I taught also had its toilets in the basement, so here again students raised their hands for permission to "go to the basement."

Once in a while after school I went home with a Finnish classmate, Elsie Harri, whose father owned a grocery store. Her mother had died, and no one was home when we got there. The first thing Elsie did when we reached their house was to fill a large glass with cold milk from the icebox and then get a handful of "store-bought" cookies from the pantry. Almost every house had a separate pantry with shelves instead of wall-hung cabinets and counters in the kitchen itself. Elsie dunked her "store-bought" cookies into that cold, delicious-looking glass of milk and ate them with great enjoyment as I, standing at the door, watched her. At home I was used to homemade cookies (albeit made with butter), not the wonderful "store-bought" kind Elsie was munching on—cookies with chocolate-covered marshmallows, with coconut topping, with sweet penuche frosting. My mouth watered as I stood watching her eat, hoping she would offer me one of those wonderful cookies, or even a bite of one. But she never did. I was too bashful to ask her for a cookie.

Not far from our house on West Harvey Street was a huge hill, the residue that piled up after iron ore was dug out. The sandpit actually formed the south boundary of many of the houses on the street just south of us. During the summers, we slid down the sandy slopes of the hill on large slabs of cardboard. In the winter, we did the same, but sliding with greater, more exciting speed and longer distances over the packed white snow. At night, safe in bed, we listened to the coyotes howl on the top of Sandypit Hill.

Ely had a Finnish Lutheran church, part of the national Finnish church organization called the Suomi Synod, Suomi being the Finnish name for Finland, and Synod meaning church council. On March 22, 1902, the Ely church had prepared its constitution and by-laws, establishing itself as *Elyn Uusi Suomalainen Evankelis Luterilainen Seurakunta* (Ely's New Finnish Evangelical Lutheran Congregation. My earliest recollection of the church is that we used the Ely Swedish Lutheran Church for Sunday School and church services and what was called the Ely Opera House on Camp Street for other church activities, besides holding Christmas and Easter programs and other religious celebrations in the upstairs of Pietilä's

Candy Kitchen on one of Ely's two main streets.

Sometime before 1925 a large basement was built on a church-owned lot, and this was then used for all the activities of the congregation. Before this basement was available, Pastori (Pastor) Antti Lepistö organized a girls' choir in which Irma and I sang. We practiced our singing in his apartment where he played the organ accompaniment for our choir. A large photograph of this unsmiling and somber choir indicates that we young Finnish girls took our singing seriously.

In Sunday school we learned to read Finnish from the *Aapinen* (ABC Book) published by the Finnish immigrant press, the Finnish Lutheran Book Concern (*Suomalais-Luterilainen Kustannusliike*) of Hancock, Michigan. The two copies I have were published in 1912 and in 1918 and are identical. Most of the *Aapinen* was written in the old German script, the illustrations drawn in 1904 and 1908. It was called the *Kuva-Aapinen, Lasten ensimmäistä opetusta varten* (The Picture ABC for Children's First Lessons). The first lessons involved the lower case (not capitalized) letters of the alphabet, with each letter presented in three ways: in German script, in the Roman or Latin alphabet, and in handwriting. These letters were printed below black-and-white illustrations with pithy statements using the letter involved. The capital letters came next, handled in the same way. After this introduction to the alphabet, which included vowel combinations, or diphthongs, the *Aapinen* also had very short anecdotes or stories. The first story consisted of only one-syllable words. The second story had only two-syllable words. Much of the other early prose was separated into syllables to help the beginning reader in pronunciation. Since Finnish is a phonetically regular language, with the major accent on the first syllable of a word, learning to read was not as difficult as it may have appeared. An example of one of the early prose pieces, translated, is:

Father and Mother

"A good child thinks like this:

"I am still very small. I am helpless. Father and Mother give me a home. From them I get care, food, and clothing. They are my parents. If I did not have a father and a mother, I would often be hungry and cold. They love me very much.

"My mother has often carried me in her arms. Many times she has led me by the hand. Often I have sat on my father's knee. They

34

*The Girls' Choir of the Finnish Evangelical
Lutheran Church of Ely, with Pastor Lepisto.
Inkeri is second from left in first row.*

comfort me when I cry. They give me what I need. They advise and guide me in everything. They talk to me about God, the Heavenly Father. They speak to me about Jesus, the children's friend.

"How can I thank them for everything? I wish to obey them, to be humble, to work hard. I wish to be kind to my brother and sisters. I wish to be kind and friendly to everyone. I wish to avoid bad words. In this way I can show my gratitude to my father and mother."

Later in the *Aapinen,* short folk tales, legends, poems, and songs appear. Some are in German script, others in the Roman alphabet. One of the folk tales, translated, is:

A Difficult Situation *(Hankala Seikka)*

"Once upon a time a man had to take a wolf, a goat, and a basket of cabbages across the river. But his boat was so small that only one of these three could be carried over at a time. This made for a difficult situation indeed. If, for example, he took the wolf first, then the goat, left alone with the cabbages, would gobble them up. He could, of course, take the goat over first, for a wolf does not eat cabbages. But whom should he take next? The wolf? Oh, no! For as soon as he left to get the cabbages, the wolf would attack the goat. If he took the cabbages next, then the goat would gobble up the cabbages while he went to get the wolf. It was, in truth, a most difficult situation!

"Scratching his head, he pondered over his problem. All of a sudden, the solution came to him. First, he rowed over with the goat. This left the wolf with the cabbages—which he did not touch. On the second trip, he took over the cabbages, but then he took the goat with him on the return trip. On the third trip, he took over the wolf, who did not care for cabbage. And for the last trip, he went back for the goat.

"This is the way he solved his difficult problem."

Next in the *Aapinen* were the Lord's Prayer, the Creed, the Ten Commandments, the Sacrament of Baptism, Holy Communion, a Table Prayer, and various other prayers, ending with the Benediction. All the religious material is in German script, preparing us for our future study of Martin Luther's Catechism and Bible history—all in the Finnish language and also all in the old German script. In the *Aapinen,* after the prayers were two pages on mathematics—one chart on the addition of integer numbers, one through 10, the other chart on the multiplication of the same numbers. The very last page is a lesson on how to read music. So the *Aapinen* even provided lessons to prepare us for the secular world. The price of both the 1912 and 1918 *Aapinen* by mail was ten cents, plus two cents for postage.

Through the years the *Aapinen* has been rewritten, and in a 1928 and also in a 1941 edition, all the German script had disappeared in favor of the Roman alphabet. The print is larger and clearer. Some of the old stories and anecdotes are gone, as are the pages on mathematics and music. More religious material filled those pages.

As I recall, in Sunday School the work from the *Aapinen* was all oral; we did no writing. This would come later, in the church summer school. I attended for only one summer, and all I remember is that the teacher's name was Miss Piippola and that we did our writing in notebooks.

Food was often served at congregational activities in the finished basement. The women were extremely generous in bringing home-cooked food to serve. Those working in the kitchen often smiled as they were cleaning up because, as regular as clockwork, one of the women would come into the kitchen and carefully look over the leftovers to find something for "Pa's pail." Miners carried their lunches to work in metal pails and a constant challenge for the miner's wife was what to put into "Pa's pail" six days a week.

Directly across the alley from our house was the Finnish Pink Hall. It actually *was* painted pink, but we children understood it was also built and patronized by Finns with Socialist leanings. Dances were held there on Saturday nights and plays were often presented on Sundays. It must have been a wonderful place for Finns to gather for relaxation and fun. But since our parents belonged to the conservative group known as the "Church Finns," they never stepped across the alley to go to a Saturday night dance or to see a play on Sunday. I do not know whether our parents would have liked to go there but felt the Church would frown on such participation. Our parents were not religious or pietistic, so I do not think it was their beliefs per se that kept them away from Pink Hall. In fact, their going to church appeared to be as much a social activity as it was a religious experience. But as far as going to Pink Hall was concerned, the Church was exerting some social control over them. Once in a while during the daytime, we children would step into Pink Hall. It was a huge room with many rows of wooden folding chairs, and a stage at one end. It smelled of stale tobacco smoke. There was a basement where food was prepared and served for the social events.

However, we never ventured down there since we considered ourselves "outsiders."

Before 1925 most of the Finnish families living in Ely did not have telephones or own cars. The town was small enough so people could walk to most of the places they needed to go. Most Finnish women spent their days at home taking care of the children and doing their many household chores. Since very few Finnish women could speak enough English to manage in any non-Finnish situation and they had no telephones, the Finnish Stock Company, the general merchandise store, provided a real service to these house- and work-bound Finnish wives and mothers. Each morning, the store order-taker made the rounds of the Finnish homes, writing down in his order book whatever items the woman of the house needed from the store that day. In the afternoon the Finnish Stock truck chugged through the alleys, and the Finnish driver, often with a helper, also usually Finnish, delivered the order to the house. We children were seldom, except in emergencies, asked to go to the store, although otherwise we roamed freely all over the town, often to the Finnish Stock Store itself. Mr. Adam Mattola was the only order-taker I remember, a good-natured, pleasant-faced, rotund man. He always called our little sister, Betty, *Matilta* (Matilda) and always spoke to her, if not always to the rest of us children.

Since our father worked in the ore mine, he left the house early in the morning before we children were awake. At least I don't remember ever seeing him go off to work. For six days each week, he probably left by six in the morning to walk to the mine, where he often seemed to have jobs as a minor foreman supervising Finnish mine laborers. Perhaps because he had been raised on a well-to-do farm and because of these small foreman jobs, in problems involving the mine workers versus the mine owners, he was on the side of the owners. The Finns published for a time a humorous Socialist paper called *Punikki* (The Red), in one issue of which my father was ridiculed in a cartoon for siding with the mine owners and against the mine workers. This cartoon was not discussed in the family, but we children knew our parents talked about it. It was a sub rosa affair so we really never understood it.

As a protest against mining conditions and life in general in a small mining town, a number of Ely Finnish families moved to Russia before 1925. Some of them returned to Ely after several years. Evidently life there was not what they had hoped it would be. In my mind it seemed that most of the people in Ely were either Finns or Austrians, with the Austrians having the largest gardens, the most cows, and the most children. The Finns referred to an Austrian as a *pusu,* but no one seemed to know where that name originated. One sport for the Finnish women was to listen to the Austrian women as they called to each other over their backyard fences and to try to make some sense in Finnish out of what they were saying in Austrian. One example of what they heard is:

"Mee kuuhun, siell' on rauta kuumana,
Siellä vihitään Rapakkaa ja Kaisaa!"

This translates to: "Go to the moon, there the iron is hot. They're marrying Rapakka and Kaisa!"

Finnish children in Ely often drank coffee, which was not looked upon as a strictly adult drink. For a special snack, our mother would pour into our cups some hot coffee, to which we added cream and sugar. Then we buttered large soda crackers, crumbled them into the sweetened coffee, and ate the soft and tasty treat with a spoon. When I visited Finland in later years, it was not a surprise when I heard a mother remark about a small daughter, "Irmeli just loves to drink coffee," or to hear another mother say about a small son, "Anssi doesn't care for coffee at all." We were "raised" drinking coffee.

One of the most delightful, even if fleeting, experiences took place one summer, perhaps during the early summer of 1925. Either the City of Ely or the Ely School District had arranged for a recreational leader on the Lincoln School grounds. All I remember is that it was a hot day, and we were all pleasantly cool under the shade of the trees at the west end of the schoolyard. We were playing some quiet games at tables under the direction of the leader, Corinne Leino. Irma and I knew her through the church, where the Finns called her *Kaarina.* I don't remember the games or the other children, just that it was a joyous, perfect day. Somehow even time seemed suspended that afternoon.

Since most of Ely consisted of immigrants and their families, especially Finns and Austrians, foreign names per se were an accepted fact of life and we were seldom at a loss to pronounce names, regardless of national origin. The "strange" Austrian, Italian, Greek, Swedish, and Norwegian names slipped off our tongues as easily as the Finnish ones.

The wives of Finnish immigrant miners in the early 1920s did not have time for weekday "coffee-klatsching" with each other. They barely had time to exchange a few words with a neighbor woman over the back-yard fence as they hurriedly hung out the weekly wash or hoed and weeded the family garden. They were kept busy with childbearing, with child rearing, and with the generally heavy household tasks of that day. Many of them had eight to ten children and quite a few kept roomers and boarders to help make ends meet.

They washed the clothes with primitive equipment. This meant hauling in the wood from the back yard to keep the fire going in the wood-burning stove, heating all the water on top of that stove, boiling the white clothes in a large metal boiler, turning the clothes over with a long, handmade forked stick, and lifting the steaming clothes into the washtub. On a washboard slanted into the tub, they scrubbed the clothes by hand with strong bar soap, often soap they had made themselves. They lifted the clothes from the washtub and cranked them through the hand wringer into the rinsing tub, then, once again, they cranked the rinsed clothes through the hand wringer into a basket and carried the heavy bushel basket of wet clothes outside to hang them on the back-yard lines. Later in the day, and many household tasks later, they carried the dried clothes back into the house and dampened them for ironing the next day with clumsy sadirons heated on top of the stove. They cleaned their houses with simple tools—brooms, mops, scrub brushes, dust rags, which were old diapers and discarded underwear. They baked all the bread, rolls, cookies, and cakes consumed by the family and visitors, making all these from "scratch." They planted and tended the family garden, canning and preserving foods for the family larder. They prepared three meals each day plus their husband's and the boarders' lunch pails six days a week. On a foot-powered sewing machine they sewed most of the clothes for the family. They knitted socks, mittens, scarves, and hats. They patched and darned the family's clothes. To add some variety and beauty to their spare surroundings, they crocheted bedspreads, edgings on handkerchiefs, and towels. They grew and nurtured with tender care their house plants, particularly geraniums and huge, billowing ferns growing in large pots on wooden pedestals. Most of the immigrant woman's life was work, from dawn to dusk—often longer. The men worked in the iron ore mines ten hours a day, six days a week.

I have just described what I can remember from my early childhood about my mother's work days. As I finish this section on my early life in Ely, I suddenly realize that I have no memory of the physical presence or appearance of my parents during these early years. I remember things we did together, I remember our house and the Ely surroundings, but I have no picture of my parents in my mind's eye at this time. Of course, I have seen photographs of them so I know what they looked like then, but I cannot recapture their physical existence in my recollections.

Brother We'll Never Know

Our new baby has died,
And our mother is not well.
We are riding, four of us,
Father, Sister, Brother, and I,
To the cemetery just outside the town.
We ride in a long black limousine,
Owned by the town's funeral director.
A small, white coffin
Rests on our father's knees
As he sits in the back seat.
Large letters of thick, gold paper
Mark the coffin, "OUR BABY."
It is the resting place
Of the little brother we have never seen.
In the long, sleek limousine,
My sister and I sit on folding seats
In front of Father and our baby,
Amazed that we ride in such luxury
To bury a brother whom we will never know.

No Grandfathers Here

My mother is crying softly,
She cries by herself all day long.
But she does all her housework
Just as she always does.
Somehow I discover
That a letter, edged in black,
Has come from faraway Finland
To say that her father has died.
She has no time to sit and cry,
For her four small children
(A fifth is on the way)
And the chores of the household
Demand all her time and attention.
Her iron-ore miner husband
Is gone twelve hours a day,
So with only small children about,
She carries her sorrow alone.

I am only six
And do not know
What a grandfather is.
No one I know
Has a grandfather here.
They all live in faraway countries.
They live in Italy, Sweden, Finland,
And many other foreign lands.
We have no grandfathers here.

As my mother's child,
I weep because she weeps,
But I do not really understand,
For to me her father
Is but a faraway stranger
Who lived in a foreign land.
We have no grandfathers here.

Influenza and Survival

It is 1918, my sister and I both lie
In our parents' double bed.
She is four and I am three.
We are ill, but we do not seem to be in pain.
Our mother quietly enters the room
Bringing to each of us half an orange
Lightly sprinkled with sugar,
An unusual, wonderful treat.

That is all we remember
Of the great 1918 flu epidemic
When more than twenty million people died.

Years later, we would learn,
When school friends had no parents,
Or only a father *or* a mother,
That the missing parent or parents
Had all been victims
Of the world's 1918 influenza epidemic
In which we also played a minor part.

The nightmare

I lie silent in a small box,
In a coffin across the railroad tracks.
The train rushes toward me,
Hissing steam, its whistle blowing.
I strain to get out, to escape,
But I cannot move.

I am lying on an operating table,
My hands tied down with leather straps.
I strain to pull them out.
I must hurry, hurry,
For the train is approaching fast.
But I cannot move.

And so I lie on the table with my nightmare
Of death approaching at any moment,
Yet never reaching me.
I am seven years old.
The doctor is taking out my tonsils.

Annabelle Twinkletoes

The Finns knew her as Tynkelän Anni.
The few "Americans" in our neighborhood
Called her "Annabelle Twinkletoes."
She lived, for some reason unknown to us,
At the very back of her narrow lot,
Just a few feet from the alley.
Unpainted, her small house turned
To a silver gray through the years.
As a young woman, had she dreamed perhaps
That a larger house would some day be built?

As neighborhood children starved for sweets,
We visited her from time to time
For we knew she always had a store
Of round, white, candies of peppermint,
With crosses marking the top.
Known to American Finns as *vanhan pojan käntiä,*
In English this meant bachelor's candies.
She kept them hidden somewhere in her tiny bedroom.

A small wisp of a gray-haired woman,
Her thin hair braided in a sparse pigtail down her back,
She spent her days in a small, barren room
Weaving at her large loom brought from Finland
Creating colorful rugs to brighten
The floors of many of the houses
In a small, northern Minnesota town.
In her own dreary surroundings,
Anni was able to create bright and cheerful gifts
As her contribution to beauty
From her small place in the world.

Life in Virginia, Minnesota

615 Twelfth Street North, Virginia

In August, 1925, when I was nine years old, my life in Ely came to an end. We moved from our secure little Ely, a town of some 3,000, to Virginia, the Queen City of the Arrowhead, as Virginia was then called, a town of 16,000, about forty-five miles away. Friends drove our mother and us children in their car, while Father rode with the truck carrying our belongings. The car reached the house in Virginia first and, worriedly, we all waited for the truck, which was very late, to arrive. When it finally rolled up to the side door of our new house on the corner at 615 Twelfth Street North, we learned that the truck load had been too high to go under a railroad overpass, and Father and the driver had to lift off the top part of the load, carry some of our household goods to the other side of the overpass, drive under the overpass, and then reload.

    Built in 1915, our "new" house sat on a twenty-five-foot-wide lot, the average width of most lots in Virginia. The house was painted light brown with dark brown trim. It had eight rooms, four bedrooms upstairs already rented to eight Finnish workmen—miners and sawmill workers—and on the main floor were four rooms for the Waananen family. These included a large kitchen, a front room, and two bedrooms. Downstairs was a basement with a large coal bin below a window on the street side, for easy dumping of coal deliveries. The toilet was also in the basement. Now we could truly say "I have to go to the basement." One set of open stairs led to the basement from a small kitchen pantry. Our father soon removed these stairs and laid a floor in the pantry. It was too dangerous to have an open stairway in the floor of the most commonly used storage area of the kitchen. Besides, we could now store the fifty- and hundred-pound sacks of flour right on the pantry floor. Another stairway to the basement led from a two-story, glass-enclosed porch attached to the back of the house. The only problem was that this back porch was unheated so that, shivering, we had to dash quickly through that porch during Minnesota's bitter winters. Also, having the family toilet in the basement proved most embarrassing to us children when visitors had to be led through the porch, then downstairs to the toilet—doubly embarrassing during the cold winter months. We children were ashamed not to have an American bathroom, with toilet, sink, and tub, on the main floor. It was a cross I was to bear for many years.

A public sauna building filled most of the back yard, with only a small yard between the sauna and the main house. Two short sidewalks led from the sauna to the house, one to the basement's outside door and one to the side door of the house. Although there was a front door, this side door was used as the main entrance.

In the kitchen, we children were impressed most by a modern appliance, something we had never seen before—a three-burner gas plate. Until this time all our cooking and baking had been done on our wood-burning black and nickel-plated Monarch kitchen stove. To heat, cook, or bake any kind of food, to simply heat some water, always meant building a wood fire in the stove. The Monarch was placed beside this modern wonder. Now we could cook with the mere strike of a match and the turning of a gas jet. There was also a two-burner gas plate on a stand in the basement for heating the water to wash clothes. The Waananens had certainly improved their lot in his world! And in the front room there was even a telephone, an unexpected luxury.

We placed our icebox on the back porch and Father drilled a hole in the floor for the ice water to drip through to the ground. We had made another advance—no need any longer to remember to empty that often-overflowing pan under the icebox.

For storage space in the kitchen, besides the pantry, we had brought with us that versatile piece of equipment known as the kitchen cabinet, something most kitchens had. Dishes were stored on top shelves behind double glass doors and there was a small pullout bin, also at the top, for storing sugar. The metal pullout counter served as the kitchen work table and was particularly handy for kneading bread. On the right side below this counter was a drawer for silverware, another for knives and cooking spoons, and below this a large pullout bin for storing flour. Below the counter, on the other side, behind a large door, were two shelves for storing pots and pans. It truly was a marvelous contraption before the days of wall-hung kitchen cabinets and counters. Later, when we modernized our kitchen with cabinets and counters, that kitchen cabinet was moved to the basement, where it continued to serve for many years as needed storage space. Years later, after our house was sold, I learned that that wonderful, useful cabinet was immediately taken to the city dump.

Our mother and father had the bedroom next to the kitchen, and Irma and I got the front bedroom. These two rooms were separated by a large walk-through closet, the only closet on the main floor. Outdoor coats and jackets were hung on hooks in the front entry hall. Jorma and Betty now slept in the living room on the old leather-and-wood lounge Irma and I had slept on in Ely. The lounge was opened each night and was folded back each morning. If we had company in the evening, Jorma and Betty slept in our parents' bed until the company left and the lounge could be opened. In the front room were also two oak rocking chairs with leather seats and an oak "library" table with a drawer and low shelf. We must have had this furniture in Ely, but I remember only the lounge from our Ely days, the rest only after our move to Virginia.

In the inside corner of the front room stood an immense, potbellied, nickel-plated coal stove with rows of isinglass windows. Our father poured coal into the top, shook ashes out from the bottom. This stove and the kitchen Monarch, both of which were fired every morning in the winter, were our sources of heat on the main floor. On winter mornings we would grab our clothes and dress around the front-room stove—after first making a chilly dash to the basement. The same kind of potbellied stove warmed the second floor. It was near the end of the hall, which meant that not much heat was spread about to the four rented bedrooms leading off the hall. But the renters never complained. In the front, the house had a large open porch the width of the house, where we were to spend many happy summer evenings and Sunday afternoons relaxing and visiting with friends and neighbors. Life seemed simple and uncomplicated, at least to us children.

How did we come to move? Some friends of ours, the Pekka Väisänen family (American name, Peter Waisanen), had moved to Virginia from Ely and encouraged our parents to do the same. They had heard that this house, built in 1915, with a public sauna, was for sale. Our father must have come to look at it and must have been impressed by the income possibilities—money to be earned from the sauna, from the roomers, plus money from his own daily job, whatever that might prove to be. The property was owned by John Kainula, who was interested in moving, or had already moved, to a farm near by. The house cost $7,000 and we had sold our Ely bungalow for $3,000. Kainula would carry the loan himself and we would make monthly payments to him.

However, moving from Ely proved to be a traumatic experience for me. It seemed as if a large, happy part of my childhood had already passed as I confronted the new life in Virginia. I was nine and would be ten in October. For many years I missed Ely and our close friends and activities there. I kept looking back, not forward. Our parents must have, too, for we often went back to Ely for Sunday visits, and it took a long time before Virginia felt like home. I think one of the main reasons we bought our first car was so we could visit old haunts and friends left behind in Ely—especially the Porthans, the Mäenpääs on their White Iron farm, the Kivipeltos in the city of Ely but also at their Burntside Lake cabin. The Kivipeltos had built part of their cabin over the lake, resting it on high stilts giving the name, China Bay, to that part of Burntside Lake. All the cottage owners on China Bay were Finns: Manninens, Hendricksons, Koivumäkis, Palmgards, Elfvings, and later, Aholas. We loved to go to China Bay to swim, to fish, to row, to visit the Kivipeltos. Whenever we went into Ely itself, we always drove slowly past the "old" house, reviving memories of our early life there.

Since the sauna would produce income only on Saturdays, it was necessary for our father to find daily work immediately. Within the city of Virginia were two lakes, Rainy Lake and Bailey's Lake, both used as bases for sawmills and filled with floating logs. Shortly after our move, Otto got work with the Virginia and Rainy Lake Sawmill on Rainy Lake, which at the time advertised itself as the largest white pine sawmill in the world, employing over two thousand men. While Otto worked at the sawmill we had slabwood (top slices off logs) to burn in our kitchen stove. However, Otto was soon back in the iron ore mines, where he must have felt more at home and where he began to have small, foreman-type jobs as he had had in Ely. The sawmill closed in 1929, after operating for twenty years.

Our house was located on the north side of Virginia. The town itself was divided into North Side and South Side by the main street, Chestnut Street, running east and west. However, we seldom called it Chestnut Street; it was Main Street to us. A competitive spirit existed between the North Siders, or "Nortsiders" as we called ourselves, and the South Siders. Most of the residents of the North Side were immigrant families.

Besides privately owned and some rented houses, Virginia also had four of what were called mining locations, where the mining company owned the land and the houses, renting them out to mine workers and their families. These locations were built near the mine sites, so the men were able to live close to their work. Just to the east of our short street of privately owned houses was the Oliver Location. Many of the houses in the Oliver Location were snug, two-bedroom bungalows, which rented for twelve dollars a month in the 1920s and 30s. Only one Finnish family, the Hermanni Lehtos, lived in the Oliver Location, and when we visited them we always felt they had a very fine place to live, with five rooms—a living room, dining room, kitchen, two bedrooms, full bath, and a basement, plus an attractive lot. They had two children, and we, with four children, were living in four rooms. The Oliver Location also had several large, two-story houses, where some of the Oliver "bosses" lived. No immigrant families lived in these larger houses as far as I knew. On one corner of the Oliver Location was the company-built Mohami Club, a handsome building constructed by the Oliver as a social center for its men employees. Our father seldom went there, for most of those who "hung out" at the Club were English-speaking; nor was Otto used to that kind of social environment. His evenings, and our mother's, were spent at home or at Finnish social events. Each Christmas we Northside kids jammed the doors of the Mohami Club, greedily grabbing the sacks of candy the Oliver Iron Mining

51

Company passed out to us children of miners. Many of us made two or three trips through those candy lines for this treat of "free" candy. We took it, and ate it with great enjoyment, happy for the handout. For many years, this was the only candy we had at Christmastime. Yet somehow, despite our greed and our enjoyment of the candy, we had a plaguing doubt, however fleeting, about why we should be so greedy for this rare treat of candy and were we demeaned by our greed and also by the largess of the Company. But such doubts never surfaced enough to become a serious problem for us. We enjoyed the candy too much.

Some distance to the east and a little to the north was the Higgins Location, linked to the city of Virginia by a long elevated board sidewalk. We walked to the Higgins to visit friends. Many immigrant families lived there. Much farther to the south and east was the Franklin Location, which to us seemed perched at the very edge of an ore pit. Both Higgins and Franklin were outside the city proper. At the east end of Main Street was the Shaw Location, but I was not too familiar with it nor with the Franklin Location, since they were some distance away, and our mode of travel was by foot.

The junior and senior high schools and the junior college were on the South Side not too far south of Main Street, something over a mile from our house. The Washington and Jefferson grade schools were near us. On our street, three blocks long, not counting the Oliver Location, I can remember only one family with an American name, the Carpenters.

In 1925 many immigrant families, particularly on the North Side, kept cows in barns built at the back of their lots next to the alley. In good weather, the children shagged the cows to spend their days in fenced-in pastures on mining company land north of the North Side near the ore dumps. Ringing Virginia were a number of ore dumps—man-made mountains of sand, gravel, and dirt that had been cleared so the ore beneath could be mined. In the summers, I helped to shag many a neighbor's family cow to the pasture in the morning and home again at night. Only one family near us, the Sertiches, kept pigs, but since they were well-tended, the neighbors did not object.

On our short block, there were ten houses and Finnish families lived in six of them. On our side of the street were the Johannes (John) Siirola family with eight children: Irene, Hugo, Taimi, Aune, Helga, Ruth, Dorothy, and Arthur. A girl named Katharine had died in early childhood when a pile of lumber, being used to finish the building of their house, rolled over on her. A son, John, had died as a young boy. We and the Siirolas were the only church-going Finnish families out of the six. The Siirolas were more involved in the church and also more devoted to their religious beliefs and observances than we were, attending church every Sunday and even in the middle of the week. Mr. Siirola worked in the mine but also went from house to house selling Finnish books, usually books with a religious theme. Our family used to play simple card games, like *Steal the Pack, Old Maid,* and *Pig,* around the kitchen table, but when we saw the Siirolas coming we quickly quit playing since card-playing was looked upon as a sin by the church and by many of its members. The Siirola parents were strict with their children, who did not roam the streets of the North Side as freely as we did, nor were they allowed to join us in the exciting night games of *Hide and Go Seek; Run, My Good Sheep, Run,* and *Follow the Arrow.* During the days they did not often take part in our summer softball games played in the street or in an empty lot, or in our winter ice hockey games played on foot in the street intersection of Seventh Avenue and Twelfth Street. Traffic was light in those days. Only an occasional car or truck passed by, a minor inconvenience in our street games.

Next to the Siirolas lived the Marjanens (*marja* means berry) with two boys, Toivo (Hope) and Yrjö (George). Mrs. Marjanen drove their car, a most unusual skill for a Finnish immigrant woman, for any immigrant woman for that matter. In fact, she was the only Finnish immigrant woman I ever knew who drove a car. The Marjanens had a blue Essex, and we always knew when Mrs. Marjanen was driving because she kept the car in the first gear down the whole length of the alley, shifting into second and high gears only after she had driven a considerable stretch on the street. Mr. Marjanen often sat beside her—meekly, we always thought.

The last Finnish family on our side of the street was the Malmstrom family with one son, J. Arnold, and a daughter, Elvi. The Malmstrom children had left home by the time we moved to the street. J. Arnold was a popular and successful doctor in Virginia. The neighbors referred to him simply as "the doctor." To visit his parents, he stopped every day on his way to the municipal hospital on the North Side. Elvi lived out in the country north of Virginia in the Finnish community of Alango (*alanko* in Finnish means lowland). Elvi's three daughters lived with the Malmstroms when they came to go to Virginia Junior College and we became their friends.

Across the street from the Malmstroms was a Finnish *poikatalo*. Literally, the word means "boy's house," but among the Finns it came to mean a boardinghouse. Our roomers and other single men, mostly Finns, ate their meals and spent some of their leisure time in this neighborhood *poikatalo*. A few men also roomed there. The *poikatalo* soon became known by its new Finnish-English name, *poortitalo*.

Next to the *poikatalo* lived the Solomon Virta (*virta* means current or stream) family with three daughters, Taimi, Jenny, and Viola. The Virtas had a small house on the back of their lot where Vanha Hermanni (Old Herman) lived.

A Finnish widow, Mrs. Heino, whose married son lived out of town, lived next to the Virtas. Mrs. Heino's neighbors to the west and across the street from us were the Spehars, a Slovenian family with ten children. In Virginia, Slovenian was the name we used for Slavs, although most of those we knew were Croatians. The Spehars had three lots, two of which were in vegetable garden with their house on the third lot. They also had a barn with a cow. Mrs. Spehar died shortly after we moved on the street and the four youngest children were taken to the Elkhart Home for Children in Elkhart, Indiana, where they stayed until they were young adults and returned home. We knew the four well before they left, but they were strangers to us when they returned, and we were never able to bridge the gap that time and separation had made, although we remained friends with the older children. As a child, the youngest girl, Julia, had a cleft palate so we had trouble understanding her as her voice came through her nose. But when she returned from Elkhart, she spoke clearly, which made all of us neighborhood kids happy for her.

Our immediate neighbors to the east, between the Siirolas and us, were the Tingstads, a Norwegian family who spoke English. Only the father spoke with a slight foreign accent. The Tingstad children were grown and gone, but their daughter Lottie, who taught elementary school in Superior, Wisconsin, often came home on weekends and for summer vacations. She used to sit on their back stoop towel-drying her long brown hair. In fact, that was about the only time we saw or spoke to Lottie. I can see her clearly even today, drying her long hair on that stoop, and that was more than sixty years ago. For some years, Bill Perry, a grandson of the Tingstads, lived with his grandparents. Bill's left leg was much shorter than the right one, and the combined sole and heel of his left shoe was about three inches thick. Bill was thin and limped badly, but this did not slow him down one bit, and he was a real part of all our neighborhood games. We heard he was to have an operation to correct his problem, but after he left the Tingstads we hever heard from or about him. We sometimes wondered if he ever had that operation. Later a Polish family, the Meizos, from farther north in Minnesota, bought the Tingstad house.

On our side of the street between the Marjanens and the Malmstroms lived the Charles Kizenkaviches, a Polish family with six children. When Mr. Kizenkavich came to the United States in 1910, he was asked to spell out his name, *Kizienkiesicz*. Since he could not speak English, this was an impossible task for him, so his name was written as it sounded, Kizenkavich, which sometimes we neighborhood kids pronounced "kitchen cabbage." Sophie was the closest to Irma and me in age and was the one we spent the most time with. Their youngest child, Bernice, was six months old when we moved to Twelfth Street. We always called her by the Polish Bronche, with a roll or trill on the "*r*" and the final "*e*" pronounced as a short vowel. In a small upstairs bedroom, we often helped to rock Bronche to sleep in her cradle, which fascinated us—at least at first. We cranked a handle on the cradle, which then rocked on its own, but only for a short while. We took turns as crankers, sometimes getting bored and tired before little Bronche finally fell asleep and we could tiptoe back downstairs. One of Mrs. Kizenkavich's specialties was potato pancakes, which Sophie generously shared with us when she came out of the house eating them. Mrs. Kizenkavich also made sauerkraut every fall, and Sophie would sneak us down into their basement to dip out of the barrel a handful of the fermenting cabbage, still deliciously crunchy. They kept a cow in their back-yard barn, and we often helped to shag it to pasture. Their back yard was almost completely in vegetable and flower garden. The common arrangement for immigrant families' back yards was to have a narrow concrete (we called it "cement") sidewalk from the back door to the barn or shed, with both sides of the yard planted into gardens, primarily vegetable.

Mrs. Kizenkavich always wore shoes with spike heels—even when she did the house and garden work. She was a very short woman so we just thought she wore the high heels to make her look taller. Her daughter Marian, whom we all called Mary, later told me that we were right, that her mother "just wanted to be taller." Sometime after Bronche, her sixth child, was born, I heard Mrs. Kizenkavich say, with a roll of her *"r's,"* "Every year, Kriismus prazent, nodder bebi komink!"

Mr. Kizenkavich had a "good" job with the Virginia Water and Light Department and spoke better English than most of the men on the street. His work clothes were always clean, not red with ore like the clothes of most of the miners who walked home along our street. Mary played the piano with great skill and gusto, and we neighborhood girls spent many happy hours gathered around the Kizenkavich piano or ours, singing "Ramona," "Sweethearts on Parade," "I'm Dancing with Tears in My Eyes," "The Prisoner's Song," "Shine On, Shine On Harvest Moon," "Baby Face, You've Got the Cutest Little Baby Face," "When It's Springtime in the Rockies," "A Shanty in Old Shanty Town," and others. We loved singing these sentimental, romantic songs, and these were particularly happy times. Of all the families on the street, we felt the closest to the Kizenkaviches. After the Prohibition Amendment was repealed in 1933, it was at their house that Irma and I had the pleasure of sipping our first glass of wine—diluted with Seven-Up. We loved the Kizenkaviches, but we never told them.

The North Side had many of what are today known as ethnic grocery stores or businesses. However, the word "ethnic" was not in our vocabulary. Much, much later we would learn that we were "ethnics," perhaps even unmeltable.

Kitty-corner from our house was the Wierimaa Bakery where, for a special treat as a break from our homemade wheat or rye bread, we would buy an occasional loaf of synoda bread. This was a soft, flat, round, whole wheat bread with a hole in the center—this hole being a vestige from the days in Finland when baked flat breads were threaded through a pole near the ceiling of the *tupa* (cottage) for drying and storing. The saying on the Iron Range was that since this was the favorite bakery bread of the Finns, many of whom belonged to the Suomi Synod church, as good a name as any for the bread was synoda bread. In Finnish, Wierimaa is *Vierimaa* (land at the edge) and we always used the Finnish pronunciation since *Vierimaa* was much easier for us to pronounce than Wierimaa. The Wierimaas also sold a wonderful, jelly-filled, rolled-in-sugar, raised doughnut called a Bismark. Later, the Wierimaas moved into the old North Side library several blocks away, and a Slovenian, Mr. Nick Bukal, opened a general grocery store in the old bakery. Bukal owned the building.

Next to the bakery was the Ranta and Niemi store, owned by two Finnish partners. Many Finns bought their groceries here since all the clerks spoke Finnish. Just across Seventh Avenue from our house was the Work People's Trading Company, a Finnish cooperative store, very busy and very successful. It was a general merchandise store with groceries, a butcher shop, and a large dry goods section. Several times a week the clerks would run across the avenue to our house for an afternoon coffee break. Our mother would serve them her Finnish biscuits, sweet rolls, cookies, or cake. In 1936 the store's name was changed to the Virginia Cooperative Society and was absorbed into the much larger and more centrally located store close to Main Street. The building across from us then became a sausage factory for the same cooperative. The sausage factory in its turn was replaced by a large apartment building, the Sundquist Apartments.

Across the alley from us when we first moved to Virginia was a small butcher shop run by Mr. Hartikainen, who came in daily from his farm bringing the meat he had butchered. Shortly afterward, his business disappeared. A two-story combined store and second floor apartment was built on the lot, and a Slovenian couple named Bodovinitz opened a general grocery store. We neighborhood kids bought our penny candy from them. Since it was open on Sundays, Bodovinitz's also became our family's "emergency" store. In time, Ranta and Niemi dissolved their store partnership. Ranta opened a store just across the avenue from the Bodovinitzes, and Mr. Bukal put in a saloon in the old Ranta and Niemi Store. He also owned that building. Ranta's became our family's main store, where we charged the groceries and paid the bill once a month, getting a welcome bag of candy as a monthly bonus. Mr. Ranta's daughter and son-in-law eventually took over the management of the store, naming it Haurunen's Grocery after the son-in-law. Finnish was spoken here for the life of the store, which closed some years ago. Bodovinitz's store later became a television and radio repair shop.

On the next street to the north, on Thirteenth Street, was Falkowski's Grocery Store catering to the Polish people on the North Side, with Polish sausage as a specialty. We often walked to Falkowski's with the Kizenkavich girls. Next to Falkowski's was a store of the Fleck family who, as I remember, were Slovenians. Farther west on the same street was Pepelnjak's Grocery, also

Slovenian. Pepelnjak's Grocery was eventually moved to the Main Street and later went into a highly successful bakery and coffee shop business on Main Street.

On Fourteenth Street and a block east of our house was the Italian Work People's Store catering to the many Italian families nearby. We seldom bought from these other ethnic stores but went to them with friends who went there on errands for their mothers. Most immigrant families prepared and ate the food familiar from their "old country" and patronized, on the North Side, the store where their language was spoken.

A major summer activity was picking berries—mostly by the children in the neighborhood. With our pails, sandwiches, and a jug of water, we walked to the road to thumb a ride to the spot where we knew the berries grew. Drivers were generous, and we usually got a ride to the berry-picking spot without much trouble. We trudged some distance into the woods to find the berry patches. The earliest berries of the summer were wild strawberries, which grew in profusion. Later at home we ate them fresh with cream, and our mother, Lempi, made strawberry sauce, often mixed with rhubarb from our garden, and also strawberry jam. I still consider the most perfect jam the kind made from sweet, wild, Minnesota strawberries.

The second berries to be picked were raspberries. These we liked to pick the least. They sank in the pail and it took forever to get the pail filled. We much preferred picking strawberries.

Later in the summer, usually in August, northern Minnesota's most popular berry, the blueberry, was ripe for picking. This time we carried larger pails, rode farther on our thumbed rides, and hiked deeper into the woods, picking for most of the day, stopping only to eat a sandwich and drink our by-now-tepid water. We tried to pick "clean," to have as few green berries, leaves, and stems as possible in the pail. They would be easier to *perkaa* (pick over and clean) at home. How successful we felt as hot, sunburned, thirsty, and exhausted, we hauled our full pails, about ten quarts apiece, to the dusty gravel road to "bum" a ride home. How happy we were to reach home, to be refreshed by long drinks of cold water. It seemed as though we could never quench our thirst after a long, hot day of blueberry picking. After we had cleaned and washed the berries, the first reward would be blueberries with cream and sugar and the next day, blueberry pie. For many years Lempi canned at least a hundred quarts of blueberry sauce each summer to be enjoyed during the long winter, not only as a sauce but as blueberry pie. Here again we felt a sense of worth and satisfaction in being able to do what was really a difficult job, to spend many hours in the heat of the day, squatting down picking blueberries, to provide them for the family's food supply.

From time to time, especially after we owned a car, the family would go to pick berries on weekends. But by far, the immigrant families for many years depended on their children to keep the family supplied with wild berries. Lempi, our mother, also canned many quarts of store-bought peaches and pears for winter desserts. Our standard dessert for many years was fruit sauce—strawberry, raspberry, rhubarb, blueberry, peach, and pear, which became to us children a routine, boring dessert.

Working at Our Sauna

Our public sauna in Virginia covered almost our entire back lot. Since we did not have running hot water in the house, a huge boiler in the basement heated the water for the sauna and also heated the radiators in the sauna washrooms. The sauna bathers made steam by pulling on a rope attached to a water pipe with holes placed just above the radiator, thus releasing a water spray over the hot radiator, creating steam. At the back of the sauna building was a large dressing room for men and boys adjoining a large room with stools, pails, and soap for washing up. This in turn led into a steam room with long bleachers and cedar *vihtas* (switches), plus pails and soap. For families and women alone, there were two steam rooms, one on each side of the long hall leading to the men's section. There was a dressing room at each end of these two steam rooms, making a total of four private dressing rooms. When one group finished using the steam room and had retreated to the dressing room, the steam room was cleaned up, and new bathers were ushered into the other dressing room. Since the forty-hour work week was not yet in existence, Father worked in the mine on Saturdays also. In fact, it would not be until 1938 that the work week would be set at forty-four hours, later to be reduced to forty hours. For the first several years of the operation of our sauna, when Irma and I were still too young to run the sauna (we were nine and eleven), we hired some neighborhood boys to work when our father was at the mine. But before long, we children and our mother took over the running of the sauna when Otto was away at work.

Since the sauna opened at one o'clock on Saturday afternoon, we children and our mother opened it and ran it until around six p.m. when Father would take over. While he was away, Mother fired the boiler downstairs with three-foot logs delivered periodically by a nearby Finnish farmer, Mr. Jyrinki, and his sons. We piled the logs along the west side of the sauna building and hauled them downstairs as they were needed.

In the waiting room, with its wooden benches around the walls for those who had to wait their turn, Irma handed out towels, took the money, made change, escorted the family groups into the dressing rooms, and sold the pop that was cooling on ice in a round metal washtub on the waiting room floor. The cost for a sauna was twenty-five cents for an adult; this included a large towel. Maybe children were free or, at the most, ten cents. However, very few children came to the sauna with their parents. In fact, I can't remember that any came. Some people carried a cloth sauna bag with their own towels, washcloths, clean clothes, or whatever they needed.

The basement boiler sent steam to the second story of the sauna to heat the water in a large, open, circular, metal tank. My job was to open a valve on the main floor of the sauna to send steam to heat the water whenever the water in the tank cooled. I checked this from time to time by feeling a hot water pipe in the ceiling of the hallway. Special steps were built into the wall so I could reach the pipe easily. I also cleaned the four family dressing rooms and the two steam rooms. Jorma's job was to take care of the men's section. As used towels accumulated in a basket under the waiting room table, we took them to the basement, where our mother washed them, and during most of the year carried them to the attic to dry on long clotheslines. If we children weren't too busy with our sauna chores, one of us helped to carry and hang the towels in the attic. We usually took the towels down and folded them on Mondays—in time to make room for the family wash. It seemed that Monday was everybody's wash day.

After we bought a car, the sauna provided the reason for an enjoyable fall outing each year. The family would drive to a nearby evergreen forest to pick cedar for the year's supply of sauna switches. After slashing off cedar boughs for a couple of hours, we would make coffee in an old, blackened pot hung on a forked stick over an open fire and eat heartily of sandwiches, fruit, cake, and cookies. The smell of cedar pitch was strong on our hands and on the cedar boughs stacked about us. After more picking, we hauled the cedar to the car, filling the back of the car until there was only enough room for Irma, Jorma, and me to lie flat on top of the stacked cedar boughs. Betty sat in the front seat between Otto and Lempi. Often in the fall and winter evenings after supper, Otto sat in the basement making neat cedar switches for the sauna. We thought, and still think, that he made the neatest and best sauna switches we ever saw or used.

For a long time we thought sauna switches were always made of cedar, but we learned later that most Finns made them from birch.

During the first few years of operating the sauna, we would take in twenty-five to thirty dollars on a Saturday. This was considered a good "extra" income, especially since the family provided all the labor, and the other operating costs—water, heat, steam, soap—were low. Financially, the family was managing well after the 1925 move to Virginia. This made us all feel more secure. It made us feel as if we had some power and control over our daily lives. As an immigrant family living in a society where our parents were deficient in the language of the land and in many of the customs of their chosen country, we were all concerned about earning enough money to provide for our modest needs and to give us a sense of well-being so that we could find time for activities not related to earning a living. During these first years in Virginia, we were able to dress well, our mother set a good table, and we had no debts other than the mortgage on the house. We had much company; we went visiting— but always among Finns. We were able to buy a car and to go on short trips to visit Finnish friends living on the Range and in Duluth, to go swimming in Ely Lake near Eveleth, to go fishing in Lake Vermilion and Burntside. And, of course, we went to many Finnish activities in Virginia itself.

In most immigrant families on the North Side, the members worked to improve the living conditions of the family. The children shagged the cows to pasture, worked in the gardens and yards, picked berries to add variety to the family diet, and took care of the younger children in the family. The girls helped with the wash, they ironed, cleaned the house, sewed clothes for the family, and sometimes babysat in the few homes that could afford to pay a little for a baby sitter. A few "lucky" boys had paper routes from which they earned money. They seemed to be the only ones who had coins jingling in their pockets. If a family owned a business, the family members usually provided most of the labor. As I look back I realize that working in the sauna did give us children a sense of accomplishment, of satisfaction—to think that we could run the sauna and thus make a valuable contribution to the well-being of the family. That we might be victims of child labor never entered our minds.

Within many families, a pattern developed in which the older children worked in the mines, the stores, the offices, and helped the younger brothers and sisters go to the local junior college and later to teachers' colleges and also to the University down in Minneapolis.

In those days we managed on a strictly cash basis, that is, we had no money in the bank, nor under the mattress. Most of our family money lay in the drawer in the front room library table, which we considered a safe place. When the library table was given away in favor of a more modern style living room, the top drawer in the dresser in our parents' bedroom became the safe place. Furthermore, our doors were seldom locked, never in the daytime, even if no one was at home, and most often not even at night. When we did occasionally lock the back door, the one and only door key we possessed was placed under the cloth runner on top of the icebox in our enclosed, unlocked back porch. That someone could enter and rob us never entered our minds. It was a safe time.

Not a "Special" Woman

Merely a Heroine

Delicately changed into a poem, with permission and best wishes of Dr. John I. Kolehmainen, from his book The Finns in America *(Teachers College Press, Columbia University, 1968) and as quoted in Eloise Engle's* Finns in North America. *(Annapolis, Maryland, 1975).*

She bore thirteen children,
Losing three in infancy.
For forty years she served as a midwife,
Bringing 106 babies safely into the world.

To earn badly needed cash,
Her husband worked in distant logging camps.
His wife then took charge of the farm.
She hitched the horse, she plowed and harrowed.
She walked the fields
And sowed seed by hand from a dishpan.
She milked the cows and nursed the ailing stock.
She tanned hides and made footwear.
She spun her own wool and knitted garments.
She hauled food supplies from the nearest store,
A round-trip journey that took three days.
She repaired the farmhouse, raised the chimney,
Yet she found time to help her neighbors.
Once she rescued a child from a 28-foot well.

She did not look on herself as a heroine,
Or any kind of "special" woman.
But she was versatile and had abundant energy,
And she simply did what *had* to be done.

Our
Finnish Names

In the 1920s we Finns cringed and became
ashamed of our awkward Finnish names.
The girls suffered with Kerttu, Lahja, Lyyli,
Raakeli, Irja, Saima, Helmi, and Taimi.
The Americans had names like
Jean, Jane, Joan, and Nancy.
The boys struggled with Ensio, Poju, Teuvo,
Jorma, Toimi, Toivo, Urho, and Veikko.
The Americans had names like
Jim, Bob, Dick, and Bill.

How could we tell these Americans
That our names were the names of love,
And of our parents' hopes for the future?
Adored One, Songbird, Young Bud, Sonny,
The First One, Hope, Gift, Pearl, Hero,
And even Champion?

Our last names gave us the most trouble,
For we had names from Finland, like
Koivumäki, Hirvivaara, Metsäpelto,
Järvenpää,Tuomikoski, Pyylampi.
If birches grew near the house on the hill,
The family name became Koivumäki (Birch Hill).
If elks had once roamed through the high land,
The family took the name of Hirvivaara (Elk Mountain).
If the family field had been wrested from a thick forest,
The name, of course, would be Metsäpelto (Forest Field).
If the house was built at the head of a lake,
The family name became Järvenpää (Lakehead).
If the farm was near a rapids where chokecherries grew,
The name taken would be Tuomikoski (Chokecherry Rapids).

If the farm included a pond where partridges abounded,
Then Pyylampi (Partridge Pond) became the family name.

But how could we explain
All this geography, this history,
To our classmates, to our teachers
Who had last names like Brown, Jones, and Smith?

The Fate of Finnish Names in America

The immigrants and the children of immigrants absorbed the prejudices of the dominant culture which, of course, for us was the American culture. One of these American prejudices seemed to be to look down upon someone who was different from the Americans, different in looks, language, name, behavior, life style. The immigrants, but more often their children, aspired to be accepted within the mainstream of American society, and one of the ways to accomplish this was to change your name, to deny your own identity.

Many Finns became overly sensitive about their Finnish names, which seemed so easy to pronounce and were so meaningful in Finnish and yet were so difficult for Americans to pronounce or to understand. Suffering from ridicule, and tired of having to spell out a name, many changed their names to what they considered more acceptable in the American society. It was easier to pass into the American mainstream if your name wasn't too Finnish-sounding.

Some of the Finnish girls' names remembered from the days in Virginia and where possible, their English meanings, are: Aili, Aina (Constant), Aino (The Only One), Helga, Helmi (Pearl), Helvi, Hilma, Kaarina, Kyllikki, Maija, Maire, Onerva, Sirkka (Cricket) Soini, Taimi (Young Plant), Tellervo, Terttu (Flower Cluster), Toini, Tuulikki, Tytti (Little Girl), Tyyne (The Quiet One). My mother's name, Lempi, means "Love." I can remember how even we Finnish kids smiled when we first heard the name of a girl called Tytti Tuulikki Mäki.

Some of these first names were Americanized if at all possible. Kaarina became Corinne. Maija became May or Mary. Maire became Myra; Taimi, Tommie; Tellervo, Tillie, and Tyyne became Tiny. Finnish girls with the name of Aili discovered many spellings of their name, all more American than Aili, a simple, lovely Finnish name. These spellings included the Irish-sounding Aileen and Eileen and also Ailie, Aily, Ilie, Iley, Eylie, and Eyely. One girl with the beautiful name of Kaino, which means modest, shy, timid, suffered so with this Finnish first name that she had it legally changed to Kathleen, and was called Kay.

Some boys' names from Virginia were: Akseli or Aksu (Axel), Armas (Beloved), Eero, Erkki (Erik), Jussi (John), Kalle (Charles), Kauno (Handsome), Niilo, Olavi (Olaf), Onni (Good Luck), Oras (New Growth), Paavo, Reino, Risto (Christian), Santeri (Alexander), Taavetti (David), Taisto (Fighter), Taito (Talent), Tauno, Toivo (Hope), Torsti, Väinö (The Quiet One). Americanized, Niilo became Neil; Olavi, Oliver; Paavo, Paul; Reino, Ray; Toivo, Tom; Väinö, Wayne.

Some of the Finnish last names from Virginia were: Airisto; Haapaniemi (Aspen Point); Huhtala (Burned Clearing); Jaakkola (Jaakko's Place or District); Jänkkilä (Swamp or Bog); Kangas (Heath or Moor); Kaurala (Place of Oats); Keskitalo (Middle House); Ketokoski (Rapids Near a Meadow); Ketola (Meadow Place); Koivupalo (Birch Fire); Kutsi; Laakso (Valley); Lakari; Laitinen (Place on the Side); Lento (Grove); Makinen (Hilly); Mäkivirta (Hillside River); Moilanen; Niemi (Point); Pajala (The Smithy); Pajari (Boyar or Russian Noble); Perälä (Place at the Rear); Ruohoniemi (Grassy Point); Räihälä; Salo (Backwoods, Wilderness); Wäisä; Wäisänen; Wäyrynen. As many of these names indicate, last names often had geographic significance, because the name of the farm or place of residence was frequently adopted in Finland as the family name. These last names contain many vowels. Pronounced in Finnish, the names are musical, mellifluous, at least to a Finn, but American pronunciations modify these sounds. For instance, the lovely Finnish girl's name, Lahja (Gift) pronounced *Lah'ya* in Finnish, becomes *Laa ja'* in English, with the significance of the name rendered meaningless.

A few "lucky" Finns in Virginia had easy-to-pronounce last names like Erickson, Isaacson, Kangas, Johnson, Kemppi, Nelson, Ostman, Peterson, Virta, Wessman, and Wiita.

Some of the *toiskielisest* (people of other tongues) from our North Side neighborhood had last names like: Agamemnoni, Agriesti, Beystrom, Biandich, Boho, Colbassani, Cudmore, Dasovich, Devich, DiStasio, Fahlstedt, Fiori, Halliday, Harris, Hughes, Kreitzer, Larson, Maganini, Maistrovich, Miltich, Muhar, Papi, Pappone, Popelka, Salturelli, Sbardelati, Stockey, Stukel, Tscholl, Voydetich. Cudmore,

Halliday, and Harris were the only families that were not immigrant families, and I had to work to find them in the neighborhood. Hughes was an Irish name, even though we Finns thought of it as "American."

Some of the Finnish place names in Minnesota that were part of my childhood include Alango (*alanko* means lowland); Alavus (from *alavuus,* also meaning lowland, with its American name being Cherry); Esko (first called Esko's Corner commemorating the pioneer Peter Esko); Kaleva Bay and Kaleva Island (after the Finnish national epic poem, the *Kalevala*); Mäkinen (named for John Mäkinen, who had a store and ran the post office); Palo (Fire); Suomi (Finland); Toivola (Place of Hope named for Heikki Toivola, an early settler); and farther away was Topelius, named for Zachris Topelius (1818-1898), a Finland-Swedish author.

Some Finnish families changed their last names to their American equivalents. For instance, Haukka became Hawk or Hawkes; Järvi became Lake; Jarvenpää, Lakehead; Joki, River or Rivers; Karhu, Bear; Kettu or Kettunen, Fox; Kivi, Stone; Mäki, Hill; Myllysilta, Mill-bridge; Tähti or Tähtinen, Star or Starr; Talvi, Winter; Valkeapää, Whitehead; Valli, Wall; Niemi, Point; Saari, Isle or Isles; Seppi, Smith. If your name was Maija Seppi, it was much easier and more American to be known as Mary Smith instead of Maija Seppi. Lahti became Bay or Baye. I remember meeting a girl named Sylvia Baye. I didn't recognize her as a fellow Finn, which she turned out to be.

Some families who had names that seemed particularly unpronounceable in America, simply took the name of Johnson. Once I sat near two Finnish-American women in an audience, both of whom had grown up on farms in northern Minnesota, one in Embarrass, the other in Palo. When I asked what their maiden names were, they both said "Johnson," but they added that Johnson was neither one's "real" last name. I neglected to ask what their original last names were! One man, whose last name was Kukko (cock or rooster), chose the last name of Thompson. Thereafter he was always referred to as "Kukko" Thompson by the Finns! Another man, whose name in Finland was Kalle Iisakka, became Charles F. Johnson. When a woman named Ida Limnell arrived in America, she couldn't spell her last name so she just changed it to Hill—Ida Hill. Aapeli Korhonen changed his name to Abel Adams; Juhani Juttuniemi became John Nylund; Sulo Hjalmer Ollila became Saul Chalmer Olin or, more simply, S.C. Olin.

Others shortened their last names. Ayrävatanen became Ayra; Heinänen became Heinen, Hein, or even Haynes; Illikäinen, Illi; Jarvenpää, Jarven; Keskitalo, Kess; Kemppäinen, Kemp; Leppikäinen, Leppik; Kainula, Kain; Vainikainen, Vainik; Viinikka or Viinikainen, Winnick. I have a distant relative in Chicago who changed Waananen to Wanen.

Still others changed their last names to more American- sounding ones. Haapoja became Hoppe; Hämäläinen, Hamlin; Hartikainen, Hartman; Huissi, Hosmer; Järvi or Järvinen, Jarvey or Jarvis; Koski became the non-Finnish Koskey; Laaksonen, Larson; Lakari, Lackrie; Laurila, Lowry; Liimatainen, Leeman; Luukinen, Lucas or Logan; Mäki, Mackey; Manninen, Manning; Marttila, Martel; Momulainen, Mellin; Pajari, Paige; Perttula, Pete; Rasi, Ross; Tästi, Tast. Names were sometimes changed as immigrants were processed through Ellis Island. The story is told that when an immigrating Finn pronounced his name Mäki, it was written down as McKee, which it remained! Mäkelä could become McKela at Ellis Island; Pulkki or Pulkkinen could become Polk.

Many Finns dropped parts of the common -nen or -inen endings which at one time served as a diminutive, meaning son or daughter of. Ahonen became Aho. Hämäläinen could be changed to Hamalaine or Hamline; Kantonen to Kanton; Kanto to Kant; Laitinen, Laitin or Laiti; Moilanen, Moilan; Peltonen, Pelton or Pelto; Pontinen, Pontin or Ponti; Salminen, Salmi or Salmey; Salonen, Salo. Sometimes Halonen would become Halone, Pulinen, Puline; Varmanen, Warman; Wirtanen, Wirt; Wuolikainen, Kaine; Rissanen, Riss—all more American-sounding than the original Finnish name. With American-sounding names like these, you didn't have to suffer the embarrassment of spelling and respelling and pronouncing your Finnish name, or even admitting that you were Finnish.

The common ending "-la," which means place, was often dropped. Hautala became Haut; Lassila was changed to Lassi; Rintala, Rinta; Lappala, Lappa; Tapiola, Tapio; Penttilä, Pentti. When I look through a Michigan or Minnesota telephone book and run across names like Heik, Kokk, Mak, Rank, Tamm, Pent, Laht, Wain, Manni, Suik, I wonder if they originally might not have been Heikkinen, Kokkonen, Mäkinen, Rankinen, Tamminen, Penttilä, Läntelä, Wäiniö, Manninen, or Suikkanen.

In Virginia, the name Pitkänen was pronounced as if it were spelled Pitcannon. A Finnish trapper in northern Minnesota, who

70

said he was born Ainer Hallonen, was known throughout most of his life as Buck Snyder. He didn't even know how that happened. The name Käärnäsaari, went through a series of changes: first to Käärnä, and finally to Karni. Sometimes, in a jocular mood, we would say, and actually believe it, that Wayne King, the waltz king, had changed a Finnish name, Väinö Kinkkunen, to Wayne King! In reverse, when a young Finnish-American drama director, David Hamilton, assumed Finnish citizenship, he changed his last name to Hanhilammi (Goose Pond).

As late as 1948, H. L. Mencken, editor, critic, and student of the American language, was to write, "The Finns, who are neither Slav nor Teutons but Finno-Ugrians and hence allied to the Hungarian, have plenty of surnames that are quite easy for Americans to pronounce and call for no change, e.g., Ikola, Häkala, Talvio, Holsti, Irkonen, Kallar, Kesti, Zilliacas, and Kosola, but there are also others that pop the Yankee eye even when they do not strain the Yankee larynx, e.g., Koskenniemi, Sillanpää, Voionmaa, Tuomikosky, Päivärinta, Wuorijarvi, Vuolijoki, Wäänänen, and Määrälä, and these must be changed." I was taken aback when I saw our family name listed here.

Others in America, particularly actors and actresses, and people with a public image, also changed their names. For instance, Natalie Wood's "real" name was Natasha Zacharenko. Kirk Douglas was Issur Danielovitch Demsky. Ted Knight, the television star, was christened Tadeus Wladyslaw Knopka. The late Mike Todd, film producer and a husband of Elizabeth Taylor, was born Avrom Goldbogen. John Houseman, the stage and film producer, actor, and advertiser on television, was born Jacques Haussman in Bucharest, Romania. The original family name of Senator Ed Muskie of Maine was the Polish Marciszewski. Another actor in television, Karl Malden, started out as Mladen Sekulovich. The singer, Tony Bennett, was Anthony Benedetto, the name he signed on his paintings. Rita Hayworth, the actress, was Margarita Cansino. Alan Alda's father's name was Alphonse D'Abruzzo, but Alphonse changed his name to Robert Alda for the movies. The famous twins from Sioux City, Iowa, who write advice columns for newspapers as "Dear Abby" and "Ann Landers," were once Pauline Esther Friedman and Esther Pauline Friedman.

In the United States, many wished to appear American, and one way to help accomplish this was to change their names.

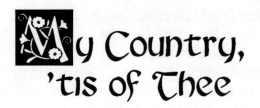y Country, 'tis of Thee

"My country, 'tis of thee,
Sweet land of liberty,
Of thee I sing."

In grade school
We sang these lines
With verve and vigor
Until we came to
"Land where my fathers died,
Land of the Pilgrims' pride."

We were immigrant children
And these lines excluded us,
For our "fathers" had died
In Finland, Austria, Sweden,
And many another country.
We looked upon ourselves
As Finns, Slavs, and Swedes,
Not as Americans.
Those Pilgrims seemed a distant folk,
As dressed in somber black and white,
They walked through the woods
To church, carrying guns.

"My native country, thee,
Land of the noble, free."
This place did not seem
To be our native country,
And we felt alien.
Although we were born here,
Our homes were foreign
In language, food, and decoration.

We didn't feel "American" at all,
At least not what we thought
"Being American" meant.

"Our fathers' God, to Thee,
Author of liberty,
To Thee we sing."
Our fathers' God
Was "Jumala," "Bog," and "Gud."
And it was to Him we prayed
And sang our songs of praise,
Not to "their" fathers' God.

We were too young,
In a way too excluded,
So it would take many years
For us to really understand
That being an American
Included much more
Than we once thought it did.

Note—The word "God" in a few other languages:
    Jumala (Finnish)
    Bog (Belorussian)
    Gud (Norwegian, Swedish, Danish)

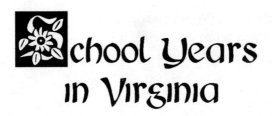

School Years in Virginia

Although we lived only a short block from the Jefferson Grade School, which looked so much like a giant chocolate cake that it was dubbed "The Chocolate Cake School," we were assigned to the Washington Grade School about three blocks away. In September 1925 I entered Washington School in the fifth grade, where the teacher was Belle Grierson, who had grown up in the nearby rural community of Iron.

One experience from that first year stands out: I was in front of the class reading out loud and came to the word "majority" which I had not seen and had never heard. In misery, I mispronounced it in many ways. Finally, Miss Grierson pronounced it correctly and I could continue. My misery stayed with me a long time.

All the pupils walked to school and then walked home for lunch at noon except for one special group, those in the fresh-air room, who were driven to school from all parts of Virginia in the school's black limousines. As far as we could understand, they were children with health problems who needed special attention and care. Just what their problems were we never really knew, but some of the students were very thin. They enjoyed a morning snack, a noon lunch, and an afternoon snack and were under the guidance of one teacher, spending their entire school day with her in the fresh-air room. Both morning and afternoon, they slept on cots in a cold room next to their study room.

Alda Papi, a North Side friend, has written to me about her experiences there: "That fresh-air room was a stigma throughout my whole life! How I hated it. I never felt healthy in there as I felt I was surrounded by sickly people. One thing I remember about that room is that we napped in the morning and also in the afternoon on cots in the coldest room. I wonder what kept us from getting pneumonia! In the afternoon they took our temperatures, and while we had the thermometers in our mouths, they would ask how many 'BMs' had we had within the past twenty-four hours. We were to reply by raising our fingers, 1, 2, 3, and so on. I didn't know what 'BM' meant and I guess I thought the more the better and raised many fingers. Goodness knows why they didn't investigate to see if I had some bowel problem. One day a girl said, 'You sure have a lot of BMs!' I asked her how many she had, and when she referred to urinating as Number 1 and BM as Number 2, I finally learned what a BM was! I laugh about that now and have told the story many times. I also remember that in the whole school year I spent in the fresh-air room I gained only half a pound."

Irma and I were still wearing homemade matching bloomers with our homemade dresses, but in Virginia we soon discovered that black sateen bloomers, worn just above the knee and showing to advantage below a girl's dress, were the thing to wear here. How we pined for a pair! I was especially envious of Ruth Brandt, who sat in front of me in the fifth grade, and whose black bloomers I could admire and envy whenever she stood up to recite, go to the pencil sharpener, or to the blackboard. Finally, Irma and I each did get a pair. What a satisfying turn of events that was!

Washington School had what served as a symbol of punishment for wrongdoing, "the rubber hose." Pupils used the term to instill fear into those who contemplated misbehaving. "Watch out, or you'll get the rubber hose!" I never understood what it actually was, or whether it was ever used. But that "rubber hose" served as an invisible promoter of good behavior in that school. Many years later, Alda Papi told me she saw it once, and it was a piece of black rubber hose.

I loved the sixth grade, the opening to all kinds of new worlds. That year I got a perfect report card, all "E's" for "Excellent." The teacher's name was Miss Olson. We seldom attached first names to adult women. They were Miss Olson, or among our Finnish friends, *Misis Mäki, Misis Leino*. Very often we never knew the first names of women who were our good friends. We simply used the *Misis* title. Our knowledge of their first names would come later when we were adults. Today I realize that there were many women whose first names I never knew. But their husbands' first names were always familiar to us.

For the seventh grade, all the pupils from the different grade schools in the town came together in what was called the Virginia Technical High School, into the junior high section of the huge building which was shared with the senior high and the junior college. The seventh and eighth graders were assigned to classes numbered One through Seven. The "brightest" kids were in the Number One classes, the next brightest in Number Two, and so on. We never knew the basis for deciding what section a pupil was to go into, nor did we even ask, for we accepted the school's decisions without question. Placement may well have been on the basis of sixth grade marks. During the two years, a pupil could be moved from one section to another, depending on performance.

I was placed in the Ones. At the first meeting of my Number One group, the teacher held up a report card remarking, "Oh, here's somebody, Ingrid Waananen, who has a perfect report card, all "E's!" I felt the remark derogatory in tone, insinuating "How is it possible for anyone to earn a perfect report card for a whole year?" I tried not to get all "A's" that year (in junior high the "E's" now changed to "A's"). I was never able to enjoy wholeheartedly being in this class.

Since it was a technical high school, there were all kinds of "shop" classes for the boys; secretarial, cooking, photography, and sewing classes for the girls. Besides well-equipped classrooms and fine teaching facilities, the school also had a big cafeteria, two large gymnasiums with running tracks circling both gyms on the second level, and a swimming pool.

In the seventh grade, besides the regular academic classes, the girls had a semester of cooking, using quality electric stoves and refrigerators, while at home most of us still cooked on a wood-burning stove and kept our food cool in an icebox with a dripping ice chunk. This cooking semester was followed by one of sewing, where we had the most modern of sewing machines, while at home we were still using foot-pedal machines built in the early 1900s. The boys had different kinds of shops, perhaps woodworking and electricity, in the seventh grade.

In the eighth grade we were exposed for one period a day to an experiential-type class. As I recall, the girls took sewing, cooking, typing, and photography, each for a specified number of weeks. The boys took printing, forging, woodworking, and electricity. We were exposed to these various "technical" classes to help us select one of them as a year-long elective in the ninth grade. Although I had no real interest in it, I selected cooking as the ninth grade elective so I could work in the school cafeteria during the tenth grade and earn a noon lunch.

Throughout our junior and senior high we took physical

education for one period each day–three days of gym, two days of swimming each week. We didn't mind the gym, but many girls intensely disliked the swimming through all the years of high school, for showering and swimming messed up their hairdos. Besides, they hated to swim. Many girls tried to get doctors' permits to be excused from swimming entirely. Others spent much time as an audience sitting on bleachers at one end of the warm and steamy pool room, after presenting excuses written from home for illness, cramps, or menstruation. These excuses were sometimes forged, for many immigrant parents could not read or write English. Although some girls were interested in swimming and in becoming good swimmers, to many it was anathema. But Virginia always fielded good swimming teams, both boys' and girls' teams. Swimming was the only sport offered girls in which they competed against teams from other Range towns. Many on these Range teams were Finns. In their regular classes, the boys swam naked and we girls wore gray, droopy, one-piece cotton suits. We hated them.

When I was in the ninth grade, a new vitality took hold of the rather dreary girls' physical education program. A young, attractive, enthusiastic teacher, Vivian Lomen, came from St. Olaf College in Northfield, Minnesota, to bring life and enthusiasm into the girls' program. She organized the regular gym classes into squads responsible for themselves. She changed our gym attire from black bloomers, black stockings with high top black tennis shoes, and white middy blouse, to a snappy green one-piece jumper suit, white anklets, and low-cut white tennis shoes. She organized an active, fun-filled Girls' Athletic Association with meetings every month. The primary team sports became soccer, field hockey, and basketball. Recreational sports were volleyball, archery, golf, badminton, and deck tennis. In the fall, for soccer and field hockey we walked to the school athletic field, later to be known as Ewens Field in honor of Dr. Harry B. Ewens, who served faithfully for many years as the Oliver Iron Mining Company doctor.

For basketball, we trudged long distances to the old Horace Mann Grade School on the far South Side and also to the Lincoln Grade School on the near North Side through winter storms and freezing cold. We never even asked why we couldn't use our own, beautiful girls' gym in the Technical High School where we had our regular gym classes. Could it have been that the boys were using that gym, besides their own, for basketball practice? In the spring it was out to the athletic field again, this time for baseball, track, archery, golf, and tennis. I think we occasionally sneaked in a little soccer and field hockey in the spring, too, since these two were the all-time favorite outdoor sports. The regular gym classes were pepped up; girls turned out in droves for the after-school sports, competition was keen, and there was great joy among us all. Basketball became the favorite sport for many of us. I wonder if Vivian Lomen ever knew what happiness she brought to the girls in the Virginia High School when she came as a fresh young college graduate. We loved her, but we didn't realize it. So we could never let her know how much she meant to us.

In 1930 the Virginia School District built a new senior high school, Roosevelt High, across the street from the old Technical High, leaving that building for the junior high and junior college to share. However, the senior high students had to dash across the street to use the two large gymnasiums, one for girls, one for boys, and also the shops and the cafeteria. During the winters we moved quickly across that cold expanse. The new high school had an Olympic-size swimming pool with bleachers along both sides. We used to joke that the District had built a swimming pool, which we facetiously called a natatorium, with a few classrooms clustered around it. Just the same, we felt it was a good school and we were proud of it.

Since I had taken cooking in ninth grade, I was eligible to work in the school cafeteria for the first semester of the tenth grade. For about an hour's work, each eligible girl worker earned a forty-cent lunch. In those days, in that cafeteria, forty cents bought a lot of food. Meat was ten or fifteen cents per generous serving, vegetables five cents, salads ten cents, bread and butter one cent, desserts five cents. Instead of using the whole forty cents for myself each day, I took twelve oranges for one cent apiece and brought them home for the family to enjoy. Mrs. Mabel Butler managed and supervised the cafeteria and except for paid adult workers in the kitchen, all the counter help consisted of the tenth-grade girls from the cooking class, all of us dressed in starched white uniforms and caps, which were fresh each Monday. I usually worked as the checker totaling each bill, as the cashier, or as a cafeteria supervisory-aide.

During the second semester of the tenth grade, I was asked to make and sell tuna salad and egg salad sandwiches in the cafeteria at ten o'clock each school morning when junior college students, some staff members, and a few senior high students came in for a snack. For this I earned the forty-cent lunch. So for one school year, I kept the family supplied with sweet, juicy oranges. I was proud to be able to do this for these were hard times. We were in the heart of the Depression.

For our lunches the rest of our high school years, Irma and I brought sandwiches from home and for one cent bought a large bowl of soup with crackers or a large mug of cocoa with crackers from the "penny line." We particularly liked the corn soup, which was never made at home. Once in a while, Irma and I would splurge and buy a five-cent dessert, especially chocolate or butterscotch pudding, or perfection rice, a "heavenly" combination of pineapple, whipping cream, and rice. Those three desserts have never tasted better than they did then in that Virginia High School cafeteria.

Throughout senior high school the intramural sports as vitalized by Vivian Lomen, particularly field hockey and basketball, were my favorite activities. But I also enjoyed the academic subjects, especially the literature and drama classes.

One of my great experiences of those years was as a student in Ralph Leyden's drama class, to have the opportunity to listen to him talk about drama, about the ideas presented in plays, and then to be transported into other worlds by his reading and interpretation of them. He also coached us in roles in a series of one-act plays the class presented to the student body on the large, well-equipped stage in the Technical High School auditorium.

He made this a tremendously exciting experience as he directed us in our various roles. In retrospect, I can say he was the finest classroom teacher in whose classes I had the privilege of sitting at Roosevelt High School. This is a particularly interesting conclusion to arrive at after all these years, since the drama class experience lasted for only one semester, yet it is as clear in my memory as if it had happened just recently. From our high school, Ralph Leyden was invited to become a member of the drama staff at Stephens College in Columbia, Missouri. He accepted. It was Virginia's great loss.

All during the junior and senior high years I had a best friend, Olga Papi, whose parents had come from Italy as mine had come from Finland. We took part in the same sports, were cheerleaders together, sat in many of the same classes, both enjoying particularly the Leyden drama class. Since we both lived on the North Side, we

Inkeri   *Olga Papi*
High School Graduation Photos

spent many hours walking home from after-school activities, talking seriously, but also laughing often. Olga was attractive, energetic, fun-loving, a serious student, and together we made the high school years happy for both of us.

Reflections on School Life

The buildings, equipment, and general facilities of the Virginia schools were excellent. The schools were large, well-equipped; the high school had a fine library. The classrooms were light and airy; there were two gymnasiums, two swimming pools. During the years I was in school in Virginia, all books, paper, even pencils and pens were free to the students. We had heard that the Hibbing High School was more resplendent than ours, that the halls were so long and wide that one almost needed roller skates to move from one class to another. The Hibbing school had been built in 1923 at a cost of four million dollars. It had a swimming pool, two gymnasiums, a carpeted auditorium with chandeliers and a pipe organ. It may well have been the most costly high school in the world.

In Virginia a few students quit school at the end of eighth or ninth grade, with a few dropping out from time to time during their senior high years, sometimes to go to work to help with the family finances if the father was disabled or had died, or to do the housework and to raise the children if the mother had died. But as a rule, most of us immigrant kids managed to graduate from high school, and many went on to further training or education beyond high school, many to become teachers. Their children's education, at least through high school, was important to the immigrant parents, most of whom had only minimal schooling in the Old Country, if they had had any. For many families, to have a child graduate from high school was an important accomplishment, a step upward for the family, especially for those parents who themselves had never had the opportunity to go to school.

I never saw any student violence in the Virginia schools, not even among the children of the so-called "undesirable" immigrant element against whom the federal government in the 1920s enacted immigration laws to restrict the influx from southern and eastern Europe. A few students may have cut up in a class to make other students laugh, but I never encountered any serious anger, rebellion, or even truancy. Generally, we had respect for the position of the teacher, giving respect even to those teachers we considered weak. Very few of the teachers I knew were of Finnish or southern European background. In looking over my years, from 1920 through 1933, spent in the Range public schools, I can remember four teachers with Finnish backgrounds: Helia Koski, the first grade teacher in Ely; a Miss Hiipakka in the Virginia elementary school, Cecelia Kettunen, the art teacher in Roosevelt High, and Esther Porthan, swimming teacher at Roosevelt High. It would take some years before Finns in any appreciable numbers would take their places in the teaching profession. Most of our teachers had what we called "American" names, names like Smith, Ruthven, Lohrey, Hinchcliff, McIlvenna, Simon, Healy, Rhoda, Graham, Silker, Orvis. A few had Scandinavian names like Olson, Johnson, Arlander, Gulbrandson.

Many of us had a sense of purpose; we were serious about our school work; we performed, perhaps too unquestioningly, and large numbers of us strove for academic achievement as it was manifested in "getting on the honor roll." Most often, the quality of teaching was high, even if many times we felt that much of it was irrelevant for the kind of people we were.

Not once in my entire school career was any mention made of the cultural wealth that might exist among the immigrants, in the subculture in which we lived when we left the schoolhouse. The history, culture, and language of the lands from which the immigrants came were ignored in the schools so that in a way our "true" identity was also ignored. We learned to deny that identity, to be ashamed of what we were, immigrant children whose native tongue was Finnish.

This was a time when knowing only one language, English, somehow made a person feel superior, more "American." Can you imagine, we were *ashamed* that we could speak two languages? We knew we were not "Americans" and because we were different, we felt inferior. It would be a feeling many of us would carry as a burden for a long time, for such scars are not easily healed.

Much of what we learned in school had no real relevance in our lives outside that school. At least we didn't see that it did. School life and life at home were two different tracks in our lives. Our hearts were in our home and Finnish social life; our minds were paying some attention to what was going on in the schoolroom. In a way, our personalities were split, and our parents couldn't help us because neither they nor we understood our dilemma, in which one foot was in Finland, the other insecurely in the U.S.A.

Our parents would not have understood what was going on in school. Few immigrant parents visited school or went to school activities, the very few to which parents were invited in those days. I think that most immigrant parents were afraid of the school; they were ashamed of their limited, broken English and felt they could not handle any confrontation with the well-educated American teacher. And I do not mean confrontation in its negative sense; even a friendly chat with the teacher was not possible.

Immigrant children usually handled their own entrance into school; the older children in the family, or the older neighbor children, brought the little ones to school on the first day. Later on, we took care of the school requirements ourselves–the registration, the selection of subjects, transfers from one school to another. We brought our report cards home; our parents looked at them and signed them. They were proud when we did well, worried if we didn't. We were expected to do well, not that this was ever discussed, however. I used to envy the students who bragged about the dollar their parents gave them for every "A" on their report cards. We would have been pleased with such remuneration, no doubt, but such a possibility never entered our minds.

I was graduated in June, 1933, as the salutatorian of the class; John Pajari, another Finn, was valedictorian. I was selected as a member of the National Honor Society and received the Lafayette Bliss Award, a ten-dollar gold piece, as the outstanding girl in the graduating class. John Pajari got the same award for the boys.

As I have been thinking about those school years, I have paged through the 1933 *Star of the North,* our class annual. Roosevelt High School graduated a class at midyear and also one in June, so the annual served both graduating classes. This 1933 edition was called a "Progress Edition," mainly concerned with the establishment of peace among nations, with peace as the goal of progress. I quote, "The growth of peace movements as such is a comparatively recent development in world history. They are, therefore, essentially products of advanced thinking and higher civilization."

We were in the throes of the Depression; many of us could not see any kind of opportunity for a productive future, yet the annual could by-pass this very obvious fact and look at the broader picture of world peace.

Little did we know that most of the boys in the 1933 classes, and some of the girls, would serve in World War II, and some would die, and peace, which that annual cherished as progress, would seem very far away.

Captain Jorma Väänänen, my brother (center, standing), in England with B-17 bomber crew during World War II. He was drafted into an armored division as a private, and later became a pilot in the Air Force. He flew many sorties over Germany and was awarded the Croix de Guerre, the French Award for heroism in battle.

The
Temperance Society

From 1919 to 1933, which included our growing up years, the Prohibition Amendment made it illegal to manufacture, sell, or transport intoxicating liquor in the United States. Some of the early Finnish immigrants had been young, unmarried men. Freed in this "new country" from the "old country" restraints of church, family, and community, they had begun to spend their free time in saloons, the one gathering place easily accessible to them. To woo the young men from these saloons, Finnish temperance societies, offering cultural and social activities and food, had been established to provide the men with a meeting place other than the saloon and also a place for social activities for families.

Immediately after moving to Virginia in 1925, our parents joined the *Valon Tuote* (Source of Light) Temperance Society, founded in 1893, with its hall in Virginia's Finntown. Finntown was just north of Main Street, near its east end. Non-Finns, not Finns, had named it Finntown. Built during 1906-07, the Temperance Hall, home of the *Valon Tuote* Society, was a huge two-story dark red brick and wood building. Finntown was also the home of both the Finnish Evangelical Lutheran Church and the Finnish Apostolic Lutheran Church.

Finnish businesses in Finntown included Mattson's Bakery, Ahlstrand's Grocery Store, the Jukola Boarding House, Ketola Furniture Store, Lofback (Lööpakka) Hardware Store, Ala Mortuary and Funeral Chapel, the Virginia Work People's Trading Store, Kolehma Confectionary and Ice Cream Parlor, the Hämäläinen Restaurant, Partanen Barber Shop, Hakala's Sauna, and finally, a short distance away, the opulent Finnish Socialist Opera House, called "Soaks' Hall" by some. For many years plays, operettas, and operas, all in Finnish, were presented here to full houses and enthusiastic audiences. Built in 1913, it was a three-story brick building with a big restaurant-meeting room, kitchen, and cloak rooms on the ground floor. On the second floor was the auditorium, decorated with frescoes and stucco work, complete with a balcony, boxes, and a large stage. On the top floor were the caretaker's apartment, a lending library, and rehearsal rooms. For the two-day dedication ceremonies, the Socialist Club's choir director composed a cantata, and Goethe's drama, "Clavigo," was performed. The box seats sold for twenty-five dollars. This Socialist Opera House became the Finnish cultural center for the entire mining region on the Iron Range. For many years there was activity in the opera house from morning to night, every day in the week—lectures, socials, dances, bazaars, music, and song.

Compared to the Opera House, the Temperance Hall was a modest structure. However, our family spent much time at the Temperance Hall, not at the Socialist Opera House. We were what came to be called "temperance," or "dry" Finns.

On the main floor of the two-story Temperance Hall were a large dining hall and a good-sized apartment for the caretakers, usually a family. To use the restrooms we went through the caretaker's kitchen, which was also used for preparing and serving the food for the Society. Upstairs on the second level was a large hall with a stage at one end and a big, potbellied, black iron stove some distance from the stage. In the winter this stove burned hot, fired with coal. Sitting on wooden folding chairs, we listened to poetry readings, choruses, solos, duets, and speeches, which were not always on prohibition or temperance matters, however. The meetings usually began and ended with group singing, most often from a songbook, *Kansan laulukirja* (Folk Song Book), containing hymns, temperance songs, folk songs, workers' songs, children's songs. The largest section of the book was devoted to folk songs which were mostly nostalgic and patriotic songs of poems about the Old Country, most of them written by Finland's outstanding poets. Our family's third edition copy was published in 1917 by the Finnish Lutheran Book Concern in Hancock, Michigan. I saw many an immigrant's eyes fill with tears as he sang these old familiar songs from the land he had left behind. Often, when the program was over, the chairs were moved to rim the walls, and now we watched our parents and their friends dancing. From time to time we tried whirling about the floor, too. After every program, and before the dancing began, coffee and a lunch were served at the long table in the downstairs dining hall. We children thought of the Society as a social club of good friends, not only as a Temperance Society crusading against the evils of intemperance. For seven years our father, Otto, served as the treasurer of the state organization of the Finnish Temperance Society. He also sang in a Society-sponsored choir. The words of their songs were typed up neatly in a small black loose-leaf notebook, a copy for each member. We were so proud that Otto's little book had a song typed in English and that he could sing it in English. I still remember its first emotional impact:

> *Somewhere the sun is shining,*
> *Somewhere the songbirds dwell.*
> *Hush, then, thy sad repining,*
> *God lives, and all is well.*
>
> Chorus
> *Somewhere, somewhere,*
> *Land of the true,*
> *Where we begin anew,*
> *Beautiful isle of Somewhere.*
>
> *Somewhere the day is longer,*
> *Somewhere the task is done,*
> *Somewhere the heart is stronger,*
> *Somewhere the guerdon won.*
>
> Chorus
> *Somewhere the load is lifted,*
> *Close by an open gate,*
> *Somewhere the clouds are rifted,*
> *Somewhere the angels wait.*
>
> Chorus

One exciting activity of the Society was the New Year's Eve lead-melting ritual. We gathered around the hot, black stove in the upstairs hall and pieces of lead were melted, then plunged into pails of cold water. "Experts" would read the solidified shapes and interpret a person's future. We children were merely spectators. No lead was melted to foretell our futures, but we enjoyed the ritual from the sidelines nevertheless.

Even though the Prohibition Amendment was in effect, some of the immigrant Italians on the North Side, for whom wine in the Old Country had been a common beverage, found it difficult to live without it. Each fall during Prohibition, late at night, trucks would deliver grapes, measured by the ton, to some Italian families so they could make their beloved wine.

Even after the Prohibition Amendment was repealed, we did not have beer, wine, or hard liquor in our house. Much later, when we children, now grown, occasionally brought alcoholic beverages home, we could sense that our parents had "guilt feelings" even while they sipped a modest glass of wine. To help Lempi's circulation in her old age, her doctor suggested that she sip about a tablespoon of whiskey each day. She could never muster the courage to go into a liquor store, so my sister Irma's husband, Henry Parsinen, kept her supplied. Years later, when my mother was visiting us, our four-year-old daughter, Kate, came into the living room, where we had company, with the news, "Grandma left her whiskey bottle on the clothes hamper in the bedroom!"

Because of my Prohibition Era and Temperance Society background, when liquor was never a part of our home life, I have even today little interest in alcohol of any kind.

The *Valon Tuote* Society slipped quietly out of existence in 1966, but in its time it served as a great social and cultural outlet for many Finns in the city of Virginia. And perhaps it even kept some of them from drinking.

The old dark Finnish Temperance Hall, which played such a great part in our family's life, is listed in the National Register of Historic Places and is known as Kaleva Hall, for in 1968 the building was purchased by the Finnish Knights and Ladies of Kaleva, two cultural societies working together and made up primarily of people of Finnish backgrounds. The Knights had been organized on a national basis in 1898 in Belt, Montana; the Ladies in 1904, in Red Lodge, Montana. The rituals of these two secret, benevolent orders, and the names of their lodges are taken from the *Kalevala,* Finland's national epic.

The Suomi Synod Church

Not only were we "temperance" or "dry" Finns, we were also "church" Finns, for in Virginia, in addition to the Temperance Society, our parents joined the Finnish Evangelical Lutheran Congregation *(Suomalainen Evankelis-Luterilainen Seurakunta)*, also located in Finntown, not far from Temperance Hall. Several houses west of this church was the Finnish Apostolic Lutheran Church. We called the worshipers there the "Holy Rollers" for we had heard that they were very emotional in their expressions of faith and friendship, although we never heard any unusual sounds of joy coming from their small, white church as we passed by on the way to our church. Members of this church were Laestadians *(Laestadialaisia)*, followers of Lars Levy Laestadius, a Swedish minister who had spearheaded a religious awakening in Sweden and northern Finland in the 1800s. The Laestadians considered the State Church of Finland too formal, regal, and sedate for any display of feelings. They encouraged a more democratic religious philosophy, used lay preachers, and rejected elaborate church rituals, preferring instead hymn singing, Bible readings, and oral confessions of sins at church services.

Our church, the Finnish Evangelical Lutheran Church in Finntown, was an extension of the State Church of Finland. The Virginia congregation had been established in 1894 and in that same year the first pastor, Henry Sarvela, was hired for ten dollars a month. Each month "solicitors," male members of the congregation, walked from house to house to collect the money to pay the pastor. Records from one month's collection in 1895 showed that $9.35 was collected. That month four families gave five cents, twenty-one gave ten cents, two gave fifteen cents, nineteen gave twenty-five cents, and four families gave fifty cents. At the time wages for laborers in the mines and sawmills, where most of the men in the congregation worked, averaged fifteen cents an hour, or $1.50 for ten hours a day of difficult, hazardous, dangerous labor. Many members had large families of eight to ten children.

In 1916 the Virginia church had become a member of the Suomi Synod, the Finnish national church organization formed in 1890 in Calumet, Michigan, to carry on the precepts of the State Church of Finland. In 1896 the Synod had opened Suomi College (*Suomi Opisto*) in Hancock, Michigan, to provide general academic training for young students and adults. Later, becoming Suomi College and Seminary (*Suomi Opisto ja Jumaluus Opillinen Seminaari*), it began to train ministers to serve its member Finnish churches in America. Until this time, the American congregations had been served by ministers trained in Finland.

In the fall of 1925, after our move to Virginia, we children went regularly to Finnish Sunday School, where the classes were carried on in the pews of the sanctuary of the church, one or two empty pews separating one class from another. The youngest children were taught in the *säkristö* (sacristy), a small room in the back of the church.

The two basic texts for the older children were Martin Luther's Small Catechism (*Martti Luterin pieni katekismus*) and a Bible History (*Raamatun historia*), the latter arranged for American Finnish children and youth by J. K. Nikander, founder and first president of Suomi College, and published in 1906. Both of these books we read in Finnish, with our 1923 editions printed in the old German script.

In 1927 both Sunday school books appeared in modern Roman type, but still in Finnish. Then in the early 1930s both books were published in the English language, with Dr. John Wargelin, then of Mountain Iron, a town close to Virginia, translating Nikander's *Bible History* in 1929. All of these were published by the Finnish Lutheran Book Concern in Hancock.

The Sunday school was conducted entirely in the Finnish language until 1932, when a class in the study of the Bible in English was begun. More English-speaking classes were added from time to time as the need arose, and for some time the Sunday School had both Finnish and English departments, with both groups attending opening exercises conducted in Finnish, after which the pupils in the English-speaking department went to the basement for their classes. In 1942 a decision was made to use English songs in the opening exercises. And in the spring of 1947 the last Finnish-speaking class was dropped when John Jaakola left Sunday School teaching.

One of the happy experiences in Sunday School was the traditional Christmas program on Christmas night when members of the classes sang Christmas songs and gave recitations, dialogues, and readings. To close the program each child was given a gift from the church, usually a large delicious apple, sometimes a beautiful, sweet, succulent orange. We thought these were wonderful gifts. It was the festive highlight of the year in the Sunday School. Years after I had left Sunday School behind, I would go with my mother to these children's Christmas programs. It was always a refreshing, joyous experience.

During the summertime, the minister conducted confirmation classes for two weeks in the church sanctuary. Around the age of fourteen, the youth of the local church, plus those from the neighboring town of Mountain Iron and from the nearby rural communities served by the Virginia pastor, spent two weeks in religious study, all in Finnish. At the end of the two weeks we were confirmed in a special church service. In this way we got to know, at least for a brief time, other Finnish young people who lived in the area served by our church. This establishment of new friendships became for many the best part of the two-week course. Short romances bloomed during this brief time.

Beginning in 1915, in order to stay on the rolls of the Virginia church, a family paid a three-dollar annual fee. This was later increased to six dollars; in 1954 it was twelve dollars. In addition, the congregation depended on free-will offerings, mostly coins as I remember, dropped into green-lined offering plates which somber ushers passed from pew to pew at church services and church programs.

The women had a strong *ompeluseura,* or "sewing circle," but in English we always used the term, "Ladies Aid."

In addition to their regular monthly meetings of spiritual and social fellowship, the Ladies' Aid frequently arranged coffee socials, bazaars, bake sales, and special dinners in the basement of the church for workers in the Finntown businesses, for friends, and for members of the church. It seemed, at least to me, as if the women were the money makers in the congregation; they kept the church solvent. In later years, especially after she was widowed, my mother spent many hours in the church kitchen with her friends, many also widows, helping to prepare and serve food to earn money for the church. Generally speaking, the woman's primary role in the church, as I saw it in the 1920s and 1930s, was a domestic one, albeit a successful money-raising one. However, some women did teach in the Sunday School. The Ladies' Aid conducted its business in Finnish. In 1938, an English-speaking Martha and Mary Guild was organized. The older immigrant women remained as the mainstays of the Ladies' Aid, and the younger, English-speaking women made up most of the membership of the Guild. These two groups worked together on a number of projects and events. I can remember many strong immigrant women leaders in the church who had talents for conducting meetings and organizing events.

The congregation depended heavily on its minister, Victor Kuusisto, and his wife Aino for leadership. From 1914 to 1918 the Reverend Mr. Kuusisto had served as the minister in both the Virginia and nearby Eveleth congregations. From 1922 to 1945, he again served the Virginia congregation. Mrs. Kuusisto served as superintendent of the Sunday School for over twenty years. She played the piano for the Sunday School and the organ for church services. At one time she also directed the church choirs. I remember her as a remarkable, talented woman who gave generously of her energy and time to further her husband's ministry in the Virginia church.

I have four of our family's hymnbooks. Two were published in the United States, two in Finland. All are small in size, with only the words, not the music. The oldest one, *Suomalainen Wirsikirja* (The Finnish Hymnbook), was published in 1918, and the other, *Siionin lauluja* (Songs of Zion), was published in 1924. Both are in German script and published by the Finnish Lutheran Book Concern in Hancock, Michigan. At the back of *Songs of Zion* is a section in English of hymns, Christmas carols, American patriotic songs, all in Roman type. We used these books for singing in the church, but I do not remember that we ever sang the English songs at the back of *Songs of Zion*. The two hymnbooks from Finland include *Suomalainen Wirsikirja* (The Finnish Hymnbook), published in Tampere, Finland in 1920 in the German script. It is exactly like the 1918 *Finnish Hymnbook* published in the United States. The second one, *Suomen evanke is Luterilaisen kirkon virsikirja* (The Hymnbook of Finland's Evangelical Lutheran Church) is in Roman type, published in 1939 in Porvoo, Finland. Our parents carried the three oldest of these books to church in the early years in Ely and all four occasionally in Virginia, for if you couldn't read music and yet knew the melodies, a book with only the words was enough. However, the Virginia church did provide hymnbooks with the music and these were available in wooden racks at the back of each pew. I was moved by the Finnish hymns, austere in both melody and word.

The sermons, delivered in Finnish, dealt much with man's sin. God seemed like a harsh and vengeful God, ready to condemn those who erred. He was Someone to be feared. I was not particularly interested in this kind of God, and my thoughts often drifted away into daydreams during the sermons. There was little in them that I could relate to; nor did I look upon myself as filled with sin. I really didn't understand what sin was. It seemed such a stern theology for a young girl who was looking for a kind and loving God. Also, as far as I could see, the pews were filled with kind, good people struggling in this alien American world, trying somehow to survive during the difficult years after immigration. They hardly seemed to need castigating for sins. They were advised to accept suffering in this world as a temporary, but yet necessary, punishment for their sins. Their reward would come in heaven. Generally, the church was too serious and strict a place for me in these early years in Virginia. Besides, Finnish was now becoming my "foreign" language since I was bombarded by English in the schools, in the streets, among my friends. Finnish seemed to have little value in this American world.

The church frowned upon card playing of any kind, dancing, going to the movies, attending plays, and the drinking of even small amounts of spirits, even after the repeal of Prohibition. However, the members had a very active social life, carried on primarily in the basement of the church, where they often gathered for fund-raising dinners, coffee socials, pasty suppers, bazaars, and meetings of the various groups within the church. And where they laughed. They were serious and somber, devout and religious upstairs, but downstairs they relaxed, told jokes, enjoyed each other's company.

We were not a religious family and at home we seldom discussed religion. Our mother had some unanswered questions about the ritual of holy communion and the divinity of Jesus. If our parents prayed, they prayed privately. But we still considered ourselves "church" Finns as opposed to "hall" and "labor" Finns, whose social activities centered primarily around the secular "Finn halls." Of course, we were "temperance hall" Finns, as were many other members of the church.

When they came from Finland, many immigrants had willingly

left behind what they considered an authoritarian State Church. In the United States they felt themselves freed from religious restraints, freed from the yoke of the State Church, which had enforced compulsory tithing, had authority over secular affairs, and maintained a powerful, dominating clergy. Many found secular organizations more attractive than the church. Our friends who were the most active in the cooperative movement, and those who had Socialist leanings were not members of the Finnish church. They seemed to shy away from the formal religious activities of the "organized" Lutheran church. Nor did they feel that the church helped workers to cope with their day-to-day problems, for the theology preached seemed to assume that it was a person's obligation to accept his God-ordained lot in life and worldly suffering. Many Finnish workers felt the church had been anti-labor, particularly during and after the 1907 iron miners' strike on the Iron Range when the church leaders took the initiative in organizing against Finnish Socialists who had taken an active part in the strike.

Records indicate that the majority of Finnish industrial workers and poor farmers remained outside the church. They never overcame their break with the State Church in the Old Country. Two out of every three Finns in America probably never resumed any church connections. Of the seven Finnish families on our short block in Virginia, only three were church members and one of these was a member in name only.

On the wall at the altar of the church was a huge painting of the Last Supper presented to the church in 1910 by the Ladies' Aid. This panoramic painting of the apostolic figures with Christ I accepted casually as a familiar object, looking at it but never thinking seriously about it, not studying the apostles, only recognizing the figures of Jesus and Judas.

One evening some of us in the Luther League, the young people's group to which Irma and I belonged for several years, were playing round games in the back room of the church. In fact, we were singing and marching through the simple, and what we considered inoffensive, "And Bingo Was His Name!" Aroused by such merriment emanating from the church, a church deacon who lived nearby came to investigate such blasphemous goings on in the House of God. However, one of the Luther League members, his neighbor, somehow managed to placate him and he left; we continued with "And Bingo Was His Name!"

Irma and I also sang in the church choir for several years and enjoyed it, especially the bus trips to sing at some of the rural churches that Pastor Kuusisto also served.

When I left home in 1935, I had never heard a service conducted in English in our church. Indeed, I had never heard a sermon in English. I was twenty years old. All my religious training had been in Finnish. I had learned, in Finnish, the Commandments, the Creeds, the prayers, the Bible stories. It was not until I left home that I learned them in English when I sporadically attended Lutheran church services conducted in English. However, for a long time after I left the Finnish church, when I prayed at night I prayed in Finnish.

In 1948 our church became the Zion Evangelical Lutheran Church (*Siionin Evankelis-Luterilainen Kirkko*). In 1962 it became a part of the Lutheran Church in America, a national organization in whose founding the Suomi Synod had shared. Zion joined the Virginia Gethsemane Lutheran Church, a congregation of Swedish origin. Beginning in 1964, the Gethsemane Church used the old Finntown Finnish church as a chapel for worship, in both Finnish and English. On February 27, 1977, the last Sunday worship service in the Finnish language closed this old Finnish worship site, for the building had been sold to the First Apostolic Lutheran congregation of Virginia, the old neighbor a few doors to the west. For eighty years, from 1897 to 1977, the old church served its Finnish worshipers. Beginning on March 13, 1977, Finnish worship service continued in the Gethsemane Church in new quarters seating fifty people.

A Finnish Unitarian Church also existed in Virginia, served by the Reverend Milma Lappala after the death in 1923 of her husband, the Reverend Risto Lappala. She had studied for the ministry at Lay College in Revere, Massachusetts, graduating in 1906. She was ordained in 1916 and became the first Finnish woman to be ordained into the ministry. However, as "good" Lutherans, we never stepped inside this liberal church although we were friends with the Lappala children, and our parents had many good friends within the Unitarian congregation.

Eventually I learned that there was still another Finnish church, also organized on a national level, the Finnish American National Evangelical Lutheran Church, organized in 1898 in Rock Springs, Wyoming. This group was completely unknown to me during my growing-up years in Ely and Virginia, Minnesota.

# Ode to
Milma Lappala

(1899-1950)

She was born
In the Finnish city
of Kuopio.
As a young girl
She starred in plays,
Collected insects,
Butterflies, and plants.
She was also influenced by Minna Canth,
An early feminist leader,
Writing in her home town.

Courageous enough
To cross the ocean alone,
She worked as a bookkeeper,
Then as a maid, in Quincy, MA, U.S.A.
Her aim, to become
A missionary in China,
Brought Milma to a Bible college,
But her liberal upbringing
Influenced her to change
To a non-sectarian school.

After graduation,
She married a fellow student.
Ever seeking a liberal theology,
Together they became ministers
In the Unitarian faith,
To serve "free-thinking" Finns
(As Milma called them)
In a small congregation
In a northern Minnesota town.
Most of its members were young,
Under the age of thirty.

After her husband's untimely death
When he was only forty,
Milma took over the ministry
Of this small congregation.
She was also left to raise
Their four children alone.
She was criticized and called
"The skirt minister"
By the conservative Finns,
Who labeled her church
 "The unadulterated church
Of the anti-Christ."

But Milma struggled onward.
She stressed the Christian ideals
Of love and compassion.
She comforted the bereaved
And affirmed life
Even in the presence of death.
Traveling by train and sleigh,
She conducted funeral services
For the dead of all faiths
And for those of no faith
At gravesites without number,
Sometimes at fifty below
In Minnesota's northern winters.

Her legacy lives on
In the hearts and minds
Of the many people
Whose lives were enriched
By the courage and vision
Of this woman pioneer.

I knew three of Milma Lappala's children. This poem was inspired by an article about Milma by Carol Hepokoski in the book Women Who Dared, The History of Finnish-American Women, *published in 1986 by the Immigration History Research Center, University of Minnesota, St. Paul, Minnesota.*

uns as
I Knew Them

In my childhood
In our small town
With three large churches
Of the Catholic faith,
We Lutheran kids
Looked with awe,
And even reverence,
At God's special women,
The Catholic nuns,
Dressed from top to bottom
In black floor-length habits
And long, black veils.
We saw them on the street,
But only occasionally.
A pure white band of innocence
Spanned their foreheads
And a stitched, spotless white coif
Extending down their cheeks
Served also as a wide collar.
These nuns, with venerable names
Like Sister Theresa, Sister Veronica,
Sister Fidelia,
Seemed to have a special link
To God, the Father,
A link that we Lutheran youths
Somehow did not seem to have.
To us, these black-clad nuns
Were truly God's holy servants
Visible on earth.

The Order Taker

Someone taps gently on the kitchen door,
"Come in, come in!"
It is the daily order taker,
The plump, pleasant man from the store,
Who now sits down and whips out his order book.
"And what would you like today, Misis?"
"Let me see, a pound of coffee beans.
I have my own grinder, you know.
Then I'll want a pound of butter, too,
And a large box of oatmeal."
"Misis, is that all for today?"
"Yes, I believe it is."
And Mr. Adam Mattola departs
To visit the other homes on Harvey Street
To get orders from the Finnish wives
Who are prisoners in their own homes,
Prisoners of their long days
Of caring for many children,
Of washing, cleaning, ironing, cooking,
Of hauling wood for the stove, of gardening,
Of sometimes caring for a family cow.
No telephones or cars are at hand.
Perhaps not even an icebox is in the kitchen
Of these modest immigrant homes.

That afternoon, the grocery truck
Chugs its noisy way up and down the alleys
Delivering the daily orders
To these women housebound by work and children.

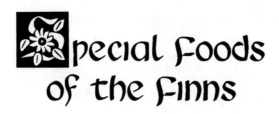

Special Foods of the Finns

Most Finnish homes always had on hand "something for coffee," most often a cardamon-flavored, sweet, yeast bread called *pulla* in Finland but called Finnish biscuit on the Iron Range. A slice of buttered fresh Finnish biscuit was especially favored with a freshly brewed cup of "egg" coffee, in which an egg was mixed with the coffee, preferably newly ground in a hand-operated grinder. This mixture was spooned into the boiling water in the coffee pot on the stove, boiled for a few minutes, and then set aside to settle before it was served. Coffee visitors often were also served *korppuja*, which were either homemade rusks baked with a butter, sugar, and cinnamon topping, or store-bought zwieback. Or they could be served open-face cheese, egg salad, or cold meat sandwiches, homemade cookies, doughnuts, or cake. Always "prepared," we welcomed coffee company at any time. After I was married it took years before I accepted it as all right to serve guests just coffee and nothing else. For years I was always "prepared."

At home our daily bread was a homemade crusty whole wheat bread baked in a pie tin as a *limppu* (a round loaf). We also usually had on hand a heavy, thick, brown hardtack made from rye flour and purchased either from the Finnish bakery or the Finnish co-op store. Our parents enjoyed it, but we children left it pretty much alone in the early years. It was too thick, too hard, and too sour for our tastes. We bought this hardtack in twelve-inch "wheels," each with a hole in the center. The term now often used for this hardtack is "crisp bread," much of it imported from the Nordic countries, Finland included. To go with the hardtack, our mother made bowls of what was called either *viiliä* or *fiiliä*, depending on what part of Finland your parents came from. It was thick, soured whole milk with a wrinkled yellow cream top, kept cool in the icebox. During the summers it was a refreshing mainstay of the noon meal. We often sprinkled sugar over the rich, creamy top.

A particularly popular supper was pea soup cooked with a ham bone, with oven-baked pancake for dessert. The oven pancake, mostly eggs, milk, and flour, baked in a large pan and then sprinkled with sugar, was especially palatable and popular.

Once in a while when a farm friend's cow or pig was butchered, we would have *verilättyjä* (blood pancakes). They were delicious, dark and crisp at the edges. Our parents enjoyed them, but just the thought of what they were made of turned us children against them. Blood pancakes eventually became the rarest of treats. Our farm friends also brought us what was known as *uunijuusto* (oven cheese), but we called it farmer cheese. It was made with the first milk from a cow that had just had a calf. The cheese was in the form of a thick, round pancake browned in the oven. It squeaked and was rubbery. We liked it.

Our regular pancakes were always made "from scratch" and were thin and large. In the early days we ate them with butter and white sugar. Only later did we learn to use syrup, which our mother made of brown sugar, water, and maple flavoring. Later on we bought Log Cabin syrup in what we thought were such intriguing log-cabin-shaped tins.

Another great favorite of the Finns was the Cousin Jack pasty borrowed from the Cornish miners, who were known as Cousin Jacks and who frequently carried pasties in their lunch pails. The wives of the Cornish miners baked chunks of flank steak (then an economy cut) in a pie-type crust folded over potatoes and onions into a half-moon shape, easy to eat as a hand-pie and good either hot or cold. From the Old Country many Finns were used to a *piirakka*, a crust usually filled with rice or potatoes, so for the Finnish immigrant housewife it was an easy and natural step to the Cousin Jack pasty, and it became a great favorite on Finnish tables and in Finnish miners' lunch pails. Nowadays less expensive cuts of beef, or even ground beef, are used, and some pork, carrots, turnips, or rutabagas may be added. A number of Iron Range bakeries sell pasties, still a great regional delicacy advertised as "a meal in itself."

When Finnish groups such as a church congregation or a temperance society held summer outings at nearby lakes, the special dish was *mojakka*, most often a soup made with freshly caught fish, milk, potatoes, onions, and black peppercorns, or it could be a rich garden-fresh vegetable and beef soup. We always thought *mojakka* was a special name brought over from Finland, but discovered that the word was unknown there until it was brought to Finland by American Finns.

One of our frequent and favorite meat dishes was what we called *lihapullia* (meatballs). Round, small, well-browned with chopped onions and a smattering of allspice, the meatballs were served in their own brown gravy over boiled or mashed potatoes. Another ground beef favorite of ours was *kaalikääryjä* (cabbage rolls). Ground beef and rice, with allspice again as the flavoring, were wrapped in cabbage leaves made soft and pliable through steaming. These were baked in the oven for a long time and were often served with baked potatoes.

A special vegetable prepared on holidays was *lanttulaatikko* (rutabaga casserole). Cooked and mashed rutabagas were mixed with eggs, cream, butter, and nutmeg and then baked.

In the early years we had few salads, but our mother did make one as the main part of a meal, *punajuurikkasalaati* (beet salad). We children did not particularly care for it but would always try to eat a little of it. The salad consisted of cut-up cooked beets, diced onions, salted herring, boiled and chopped eggs, and diced apple, all held together with dressing.

At Christmastime our parents' great delight came on Christmas Eve. After we had all had our saunas and the tree had been trimmed, they enjoyed *lipeäkalaa* (lutefisk, or cod) smothered in white sauce, laced with black pepper, and served with boiled potatoes. Our mother had soaked the stiff lutefisk in a pail of water for several days to soften it. We children didn't care for this. I can't remember what we ate instead, perhaps meatballs.

Another great treat, a very special pastry called a *torttu* (tart), was prepared for Christmastime. These were usually saved for Christmas company, when we children could enjoy them too. Sweetened, cooked prune pulp was placed in the center of a small, rolled-out square of rich, flaky pastry. The pastry square was then cut diagonally at the corners and the pastry folded over the prune paste into a star-like shape, and baked. The great *torttu* artist in my memory was Mary Kivipelto of Ely. Her *torttus* were the lightest, the flakiest, the most delicious to come out of any Finnish kitchen I knew of.

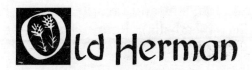ld Herman

He lived quietly in a small, two-room house
In the back yard of a house on our street.
He seemed old to us children,
But his age was never a matter of concern.
He was known only as *Vanha Hermanni,*
Old Herman.

We never knew his last name,
Nor even thought to ask what it might be.
We children never wondered
What his past might have been:
Why he had left the Old Country,
Or whom he had left behind
To live a solitary life in a small house
In someone else's back yard.

He was just Old Herman,
A part of our daily life,
And one who knocked gently
On the back doors of the Finnish homes nearby
For his morning and afternoon coffee.

When he was seated at our kitchen table,
And my mother had poured hot coffee into his cup,
Old Herman would pour some into his saucer,
Always a generous amount,
And, with trembling hand, lift it
To the lump of sugar anchored between his front teeth,
To suck the coffee sweetened through the sugar.
We always watched with considerable awe,
Afraid his shaking hand would spill the coffee
On his pants or on our tablecloth.
But we never saw Old Herman
Spill a single drop.

The 1920s and Early 1930s

We were growing up in the 1920s, in the era of the free-spirited flapper (defined as a young woman who behaved in a manner free of traditional social and moral restraints), the big-name dance bands, the popular public dance halls, and the illegal speak-easy. It was the great Jazz Age, only we didn't know it. If we had, we might have paid more attention. A Minnesota author, F. Scott Fitzgerald, who was born in St. Paul in 1896, was to write about it, about the gay, mad, bootleg-gin-drinking young people.

In 1922 a story in the *Hibbing Daily Tribune* admonished, "Those who desire to dance the shimmy will have to confine their activities to some place other than Hibbing, says Mrs. Pritchard, the policewoman who posted regulations in all the public dance halls of Hibbing this week. Neither will cheek-to-cheek dancing be tolerated. This means that dancers must hold their partners at a distance."

Before this, cheek-to-cheek dancing, sometimes even closer, was the rule and not the exception. The "shimmy" was an American ragtime dance marked by shaking the hips and shoulders.

We were children, living in a rather narrowly prescribed environment of home, neighborhood, school, and church. We did dance the Charleston, however, on the sidewalks, our usual playgrounds. Later we learned to dance a snappy fox trot at the school dances.

The most daring of the Finnish women and young girls bobbed their hair, many against the wishes of their husbands or fathers. Bobbing hair was looked upon as highly improper, if not downright risqué, for if a woman or girl bobbed her hair, she might just smoke cigarettes, or even drink bootleg gin. When our mother just mentioned getting her hair bobbed, we children set up such a clamor against it that in her lifetime she never bobbed her hair. And she lived to be eighty-nine!

We saw the older young people riding around in open flivvers and tin lizzies. We heard of such things as hip flasks for booze— flasks shaped to fit the contours of the hip. We went to the silent films for ten cents a child, and we devotedly pasted into scrapbooks, from newspapers and movie magazines, the pictures of Mary Pickford, Buddy Rogers, Colleen Moore, Clara Bow, Marie Dressler, Charlie Chaplin, Marie Prevost, Buster Keaton, Harold Lloyd, Rudolph Valentino, and Douglas Fairbanks, Sr. They were our world of comedy, fantasy, and romantic love.

In 1928 we saw our first picture with sound, *The Jazz Singer,* with Al Jolson. Technicolor came later, in 1932, to usher in the heyday and golden age of Hollywood, its thousands of movies, and its big-name stars. Bette Davis and Katharine Hepburn would become our favorite dramatic actresses. We adored them. Other names to remember include Clark Gable, Paul Muni, Spencer Tracy, Humphrey Bogart, Cary Grant, Claudette Colbert, Robert Young, Maurice Chevalier, Jeanette MacDonald and Nelson Eddy, Fred Astaire and Ginger Rogers, Greta Garbo, Judy Garland, Charles Laughton, Spencer Tracy, Gary Cooper, Leslie Howard, and Fredric March. To us they pictured a fantasy world, a dream life. We didn't relate the movies to our own lives; they were our escape, and we took them seriously. Going to the movies was an important event, not just a casual affair. We looked at the movies with innocent eyes, uncritically. Sitting in the movie theater, anticipating what would unfold on that silver screen filled us with satisfaction, contentment. We were sharing in an American phenomenon, the Hollywood motion picture, and we were completely taken in by it. I believe we felt most "American" sitting in those darkened theaters in the late 1920s and early 1930s watching the screen stories unfold. Our parents, however, never went to these movies. Their limited English language skills must have deterred them; such entertainment was not part of their life-style. Later, they would go to Finnish films imported from Finland and shown in the various Finn halls. We children never went to the Finnish movies, for Finland at that time was of little interest to us. We were captives of Hollywood.

A great pioneering feat occurred on May 20, 1927, when a twenty-five-year-old pilot, Charles Lindbergh, from Little Falls, Minnesota, with his single-engine plane, the *Spirit of St. Louis,* and with a ton of fuel around him, flew alone from New York City to Paris in thirty-three hours, the first person to fly alone non-stop across the Atlantic, an "impossible" 3,600 miles. The whole world celebrated this great accomplishment. We shared in it through the newspapers, the newsreels at the movies, and family discussions. We were especially proud that he was a Minnesotan, our "Lone Eagle."

Later, we suffered with the Lindberghs when 20-month-old Charles Lindbergh, Jr., was kidnapped and killed in March, 1932. We also suffered with the Hauptmanns when Bruno Hauptmann was tried, found guilty, and executed for the murder.

We heard about "Scarface" Al Capone, the gang leader from Chicago, and about John Dillinger, the notorious bank robber and killer, "Public Enemy Number One." Other well-known outlaws had names like "Baby Face" Nelson, "Pretty Boy" Floyd. But violent crime was something far removed from our daily lives. We knew about speak-easies, although we never saw one except in the movies. Our sources of information were the daily newspaper, the newsreels at the movies, and discussions by our parents and their friends. Our family had no radio.

In 1927 we bought our first car, a second-hand, four-door touring car, a 1924 Buick, with "California" side curtains to snap on when it rained or when the wind got too chilly. In that same year we learned that the Model T Ford would no longer be made, that it would be replaced by the Model A, priced at $385. But we were not in the market for a new car, at least not yet.

Otto was forty-four years old when he learned to drive, and for a long time he remained an excited, erratic driver, sometimes knocking the side of the garage upon entering, sometimes hitting the tree across the street as he backed out of the garage too fast, and occasionally losing some control on sharp curves on the gravel roads we traveled outside of town. Our next car was a second-hand, blue, two-door, 1926 Buick sedan, a roomy car, fine for hauling our cedar boughs from the woods for the sauna switches. Sometime later, we bought a large, green 1928 Hudson, again second-hand. We were proud of that car; it cost a lot, $300. We bought it from a man named Hendrickson in neighboring Eveleth.

In the 1920s and early 1930s, we never used our car during the winter months. In the late fall, the water was drained from the radiator, the battery was removed and hauled down into the basement, the car was put on blocks in the garage and forgotten until spring. Cars had no heaters so you bundled up in blankets if you were foolhardy enough to travel at all in cold weather. The windshield wiper, located only on the driver's side, was operated by hand. Often the person sitting beside the driver would move the wiper back and forth so the driver could concentrate on the driving. If at all possible, driving in the rain was avoided. The fastest automobile speed within our comprehension was sixty miles an hour. In fact, "sixty per" became the term to indicate the very highest speed we could imagine. If a speeding car whizzed past our car on the road, and we watched that daredevil of a driver fade into the distance, someone was bound to exclaim, "He must be going sixty per!"

It would not be until the fall of 1936 that we would buy our first new car, a 1937 four-door, gray Dodge sedan. It cost $850. Our brother, Jorma, helped to pay for it as he was now working in the same mine as Otto.

In 1928 President Calvin Coolidge, who was the Republican president from 1923-1929, visited Virginia, and the whole town lined the Main Street to watch the President and Mrs. Coolidge glide past in an open touring car. My only remark to my mother was, "You look just like Mrs. Coolidge!" In my eyes she did, for they were both dark-haired and wore their hair in the same style. Politically, my parents were conservative, voting the Republican ticket. Perhaps Otto's being a well-to-do landowner's son in Finland contributed to his conservatism. And, of course, since he frequently served as a foreman in the mines, he must have felt that he had been treated well by the mining companies. He, no doubt, looked upon the mining company as a benefactor, not as an exploiter, as so many Finnish miners began to consider these companies.

Since our parents were Republicans, we children naturally sided with the Republicans. When, in 1928, the Catholic Democrat from New York, the derby-hatted, cigar-smoking Al Smith, was running for president against Herbert Hoover, the Protestant Republican, one of our favorite rallying cries was, "What can only one Smith do, if it takes two to make a cough drop?" In those days, the Catholics and the Lutherans were religious adversaries. I recall that although many of us Lutherans went to masses with our Catholic friends, these Catholic friends never came to a service in our Lutheran churches. They just said the priest wouldn't let them.

Although many Finnish miners and lumberjacks in Minnesota were active in the labor movement, I do not think Otto took part in any action on behalf of the miners. In fact, he was ridiculed in a cartoon in one issue of the *Punikki* (The Red), a popular Finnish humor sheet with a pronounced Socialist bias, for siding with the mine owners instead of with the miners with whom he worked and most of whom were Finns. I have tried to locate this issue of *Punikki* but so far have failed. As children, we heard some talk about the cartoon, but we never understood what it all meant.

Like my father, most of the Finnish men on the Range worked in mining. In the open pit mines many Finns were day laborers who stripped away the overburden of glacial drift, rocks, pine needles, and soil in order to uncover the rich ore deposits lying underneath. Without language skills, without any training, the open pits were one place the unskilled Finnish laborers found work they were able to do. By drilling and blasting, the skilled miners then loosened the ore, which giant steam shovels scooped into open railway cars for shipment to the ore docks on Lake Superior. Many Finnish men also worked in underground mines under what were often dangerous conditions.

Wages were low; many of the foreign-born mine employees earned between $10 and $15 per week for ten hours of labor each day, six days a week. From these wages the cost of explosives, fuses, and caps were deducted, leaving even less in the pay envelope. Most immigrant workers, not only the Finnish ones, were caught on the bottom rung of the economic ladder; they were treated harshly on the job, overworked, pressured to produce more and more iron ore. Many men were injured, maimed, or killed from falling rocks, cave-ins, floods, misuse of explosives, or general carelessness, sometimes including drunkenness. A number of children on the North Side of Virginia had no fathers; they had been killed in mine accidents; other miner fathers bore scars from mine accidents.

On July 19, 1907, the miners on the Mesabi Range, which included the Virginia mines, asked the Oliver Mining Company for an eight-hour day, an end to bribes and bonuses, and a day's wage of at least $2.50 for open-pit miners and $3.00 for those working in the dangerous underground mines. However, the Oliver refused to talk with them. Instead, it fired three-hundred miners, and then brought in more than a thousand strikebreakers, mostly Montenegrins and Croatians who had just arrived on the East Coast from the Old Country. They did not understand that they were strikebreakers. Some of them, when they realized that they were scabs, quit their jobs. The strike lasted two months and at the end, many striking Finnish miners were blacklisted and barred from re-employment in the mines. Some went back to Finland, some moved to other states, others went to northern lumber camps, many moved to farms in northeastern Minnesota.

Nine years later, in 1916, the Iron Range miners struck again against the mining companies. This time they also asked for an eight-hour day for all miners, no Saturday night work shifts, pay raises to raise daily pay to $2.75 for open-pit miners and to $3.00 and $3.50 for underground miners. Miners were earning about $2.00 a day and worked only seven months of the year because of the severe winters and frozen ground. They also asked for payment twice a month instead of once a month so they wouldn't have to charge at the company store. They wanted an end to contract pay in which the miners were paid only for the ore they dug out, not for the time they put in. The miners claimed that wage contracts were often changed by the companies, and less was paid per ton than had been agreed upon. The miners lost again. Once more, many Finns lost their mining jobs; again, some moved to farms; others went to work in lumber camps; still others moved away from Minnesota.

But these strikes were ancient history by the time I was growing up; our parents never spoke about them, nor did their friends, at least not within earshot of us children. It was only later that I even heard about these two strikes and the active part the Finnish miners played in them. I can only conclude that talk about striking Finnish miners must have been tabooed or banned in the Finnish community, at least in our conservative church community. It is my understanding that the miners considered the Suomi Synod Church to be anti-labor during the strikes.

Fortunately for them, many of the Finnish miners and their families, after both strikes, were able to move to northeastern Minnesota farms. Landless in Finland, many an immigrant cherished the dream of owning a farm in the United States. Farm life, even on the poor cutover, rocky land in northeastern Minnesota, seemed inviting when compared to the dangerous work in the mines. The Finns had a saying, *Oma tupa, oma lupa* (When you have your own place, you are your own boss). These farms must have served as a safety valve for the blacklisted miners, allowing them to make a new start in America, even though eventually many of the farms proved to be unsuccessful economically.

In summertime, in June, occurred the great northern Minnesota Finnish Midsummer Festival, the *Juhannusjuhla,* St. John's Day, that in pagan Finland honored the sun gods, but in Minnesota celebrated the return of the long-awaited summer. Finns came from all over the state to this outdoor festival, which each year was held in a selected city in its park or on its lakeshore. They came to meet old friends, to make new friends, to celebrate being Finns, to remember and commemorate Finland. Finns of all political and religious persuasions came for the *Juhla*. The "labor," "temperance," and "church" Finns, plus those with no group affiliations, came to mingle and to celebrate their common bonds of heritage. It was like the gathering of a large, talkative clan, Finns in a jovial, holiday mood.

In my memory it remains as a one-day festival, a Sunday fest, with bands, choruses, rousing speeches, poetry reading, food. We children played with old friends from other towns and farms and met new friends. On that day we were able to indulge in the rare luxury of an ice cream cone and a bottle of pop, each for five cents. We hardly heard the music, the speeches, the poetry readings, for we strayed from the main audience. We lingered at its outer edges. If the festival was beside a lake, we hovered about the shore. We were at the festival, yet we were not really a part of it. However, we recognized it as a great gathering day for the adults.

Later, the festival was extended to two days, Saturday and Sunday. Athletic contests, including the 100-yard dash, half-mile run, shotput, discus throw, broad jump, were run on Saturday, mostly for adults, but some for boys and girls. A festive banquet followed that night, with audience singing, poetry readings, choruses, patriotic and nostalgic speeches. This banquet, in later years, was followed by a dance with a live orchestra. On Sunday morning, after early church services for the faithful, the festival continued outdoors with more music and song, more poetry, more speeches, and a splendid dinner at noon. The celebration would end with a play or concert on Sunday night. And thus refreshed, the Finns returned to their homes to carry on their own community life, but already looking forward to the next summer's *Juhannusjuhla*.

Every so often our mother took part in an ancient ritual brought from Finland, that of bloodletting, a process of thinning the blood or ridding the body of impurities. From time to time, Mrs. Holmstrom, the North Side's "resident" Finnish *kuppaaja* (bloodletter or cupper), would arrive, black bag in hand, and she and our mother would disappear into the heated sauna. Later, they would emerge with our mother tired, yet relaxed, seemingly rereshed from both the cupping and the sauna with small red cuts on her legs, at least that is all we saw. Although we never watched Mrs. Holmstrom at work, we knew that with a small, sharp scalpel she made a cut in the flesh, placed the large open end of a small cowhorn (*kuppaussarvi*) over the cut and with her mouth at the small opening of the horn, sucked blood into the horn. This small end of the horn was covered with a calf bladder, or something similar, so the blood did not flow into her mouth. Whether the cupping was done elsewhere on our mother's body, we did not know. This cupping must have given our mother relief, since every now and then on a Saturday, Mrs. Holmstrom, with her black bag, showed up at our back door.

In our family the standard greeting to friends and the very few relatives we had in this country and the standard leave-taking from them was a warm handshake. The greeting handshake was usually accompanied by the words, *Tervetuloa* (Welcome) or *Terveisiä* (Greetings). The departure handshake was accompanied by *Hyvästi* (Good-bye). It would not be until after the 1939-1940 Winter War with Russia that *Näkemiin* (See you again), akin to the German *Auf wiedersehen*, would prevail over *Hyvästi*. I have understood that saying *Hyvästi*, or Good-bye, to a Finnish soldier as he left for the battlefront, and his saying it, also, appeared too final and pessimistic a farewell. *Näkemiin* ("See you again" or "Good-bye for the present") somehow softened the impact of the pain of departure, even though all the participants knew it could well prove to be the final good-bye. *Näkemiin* crossed the Atlantic Ocean and became the favored farewell among Finnish people in the United States.

In our childhood, our family was not a demonstrative one. I never saw our mother and father kiss or hug each other. Their Finland backgrounds simply did not include these expressions of affection. I believe they looked upon kissing as an American custom. I have seen a short documentary on modern farm life in Finland in which the father had spent most of the winter months away from home working in the woods as a lumberjack. When he walked into the farmyard, his two children and his wife each greeted him with a handshake, but by their expressions one recognized that they were all extremely happy that he was home again. Nor did we children hug or kiss each other or our parents. We would have been embarrassed to do so. Although we four children were good friends, cared about one another, and supported each other whenever the need arose, we did not display our feelings with kissing and hugging. Most of our experiences with various expressions of affection were vicarious, second hand, that is, we saw them in the movies. Here we saw expressions of romantic love, American style. I do not recall kissing my parents until the time came for me to leave home for the

University down in Minneapolis, and even then it was not an easy thing to do. But once the ice was broken, affectionate greetings and farewells no longer posed any problems. Later we children were to engage in necking (at least that's what we called it then) with members of the opposite sex. But, believe me, we never talked about this to the family at home. It was a completely private affair.

In 1928, for the first time, we had a visit from our closest relatives in the United States, our Uncle Uuno and his family, who drove in their open touring car to Minnesota from Cincinnati, Ohio. Lempi and her only brother, Uuno, had been the only Helander children to migrate to America; he had come in 1910, Lempi in 1911. While still in Finland, Uuno had changed his last name from the Swedish Helander to the Finnish Salovaara (Wilderness Hill). In the early 1900s patriotic fervor for things and names Finnish was sweeping over the land that had been a Swedish province for years and was now a Russian grand duchy. The Finns were feeling increasingly oppressed under ever more autocratic czarist regimes. In 1906, in a single day, about 100,000 Finns in Finland changed their Swedish names to Finnish ones, even inventing some completely new names. They no longer wished to be known as Swedes, nor did they look upon themselves as Russians. They wanted to be Finns. Uuno was one among this large group. Salovaara would be the name Uuno and his American children and grandchildren would use. Lempi kept the family name of Helander until she married.

Continuing in the work of his grandfather and father, Uuno had first worked as a tailor in New York City and then in Chicago, where he was one of several dozen tailors and seamstresses in a large tailor shop. In 1915 he married Sylvi Huissi, whom he had met at a Finnish Fourth of July picnic in Waukegan, Illinois. When Sylvi was thirteen, she and her fifteen-year-old brother, Wilhelm, had come from Tampere, Finland, to join their father and their stepmother in Racine, Wisconsin. Their two younger half-brothers had remained temporarily in Finland with their stepmother's family; the plan was for them to join their parents in America as soon as possible. However, shortly after Sylvi's and her brother's arrival in Racine, their stepmother died of typhoid fever. In Racine, Sylvi had first worked for a dressmaker for six months without pay, after which she was paid three dollars a week. Learning from a Finnish girl friend how well-paid domestic workers were in Chicago, Sylvi left Racine for Chicago and found a job at seven dollars a week doing the housework for a family with two children, who lived in the Kenilworth suburb of Chicago. She had her own room, her own bath, and excellent food. Her employers liked her; they treated her like a member of their family, included her in their activities, and took her with them to their country club. Having had success as a dressmaker, Sylvi knew how to dress well. She was an attractive young woman. No wonder Uuno had fallen in love with her. After their marriage in 1915, they had settled in an apartment on Riverside Drive in Chicago, and lived well. On October 7, 1916, their son, Jorma Julius, was born.

In 1917 the effects of World War I had ruined the tailoring shop where Uuno worked in Chicago and the family moved to Cincinnati, Ohio. Here Uuno continued to develop his tailoring craft and built up a thriving business, sending money to banks in Finland with the intent of returning some day to his native land. But in time, factory mass production of men's clothing undermined his hand-tailoring business, the Finnish banks failed, and he was ultimately reduced to a small one-man tailor shop. Two other children were born, Irene Elizabeth in 1917, and Viola Eleanore in 1922.

In their home in Cincinnati, the Salovaaras had first spoken mostly Finnish, with their son Jorma speaking only Finnish until he entered school. However, as the years passed, English developed into the language used in their home. The neighbors and other acquaintances were not Finnish. The two dozen or so Finnish families in Cincinnati were scattered about in the city. When the Salovaaras got together with them, Finnish was the language spoken among the adults. But even in these Finnish groups, the children were spoken to in English, so through the years the children lost their ability to use the Finnish language. With so few Finns living in Cincinnati, Finnish societies were not organized as they were in communities where many Finns had settled.

Since their mother had died in Racine, Sylvi's two young half-brothers, who had been left in Finland, were never to come to the United States. The older brother died in Finland's 1918 Civil War, and the younger one had been wounded in the same war.

So here they were, the Salovaara family in 1928, visiting us in Virginia, Minnesota. We children were quite awed by these "Eastern" cousins, who spoke with an accent we had never heard. We were also impressed by their vocabularies, which appeared much more sophisticated than ours. Cousin Irene was only eleven years old, yet she spoke about having to change her "perspective" on life. We felt immature in comparison. These cousins could not speak Finnish, which made them seem even more "American" in our eyes. But we had a lot of fun with them. They enjoyed the Saturday saunas, where Irene and Viola amazed us by dumping pails of ice-cold water over their heads. Our two families drove in our touring cars to pick blueberries, to visit the nearby lakes for swimming and fishing. Their visit was great fun for us all.

The Great Depression Hits

In 1929, four years after we had moved to Virginia, the Waananens were doing quite well financially, with income from Otto's job in the mine, the Saturday money from the sauna, the money from the upstairs roomers, with all the work done by the family.

The children were growing up, doing well in school. We had good neighbors, a large circle of friends, many activities.

We had nice furniture. A fine, nine-by-twelve wool rug lay on the front room floor. A dark gray velour davenport with a matching chair had replaced the old oak and leather *lounssi* and the wooden rocking chairs. The sturdy library table was gone, with several small tables taking its place. There was money for "extras." We had bought a brand new Kimball piano for $500, and my sister Irma was taking piano lessons on the South Side from Mrs. Anthony, whose night-shift policeman husband slept during the day so Irma became an expert on the use of the soft pedal. Later, she took lessons from the Lombardi Conservatory of Music out of Hibbing and appeared in their recitals. We had a second-hand car, our mother had a nice fur coat, and everybody's health was good. The family had a sense of well-being.

We weren't obsessively concerned with income simply because we now had a good income. Our days were no longer filled with a struggle to make ends meet. There was time for family excursions in the car, mostly for visiting friends on farms and in Ely, and for fishing trips. There was money so we children could go to the "important" movies in downtown Virginia and could buy a bag of popcorn, too. It was a time for entertaining friends, for being entertained by them. We were active in the church, in the temperance society; we children were busy with school and with our friends. Life was safe, secure. The family, prospering, had a sense of well-being.

But after the stock market crash of 1929, everything changed. The Great Depression began. The sauna business began to drop off, for people no longer had quarters to pay for a sauna. Soon it was no longer profitable to keep the sauna running and we closed its doors. Our roomers disappeared one by one as they lost their jobs. One of them left his IWW (Industrial Workers of the World) papers behind in our attic. We tossed them away without even looking through them. As "church" Finns, we knew they were suspect. What other memorabilia that our roomers left behind did we toss out? The boardinghouse across the street closed; a Norwegian family moved into the building. The Oliver Iron Mining Company, or "The Oliver" as we called it, offered the miners work for five days each month at five dollars a day, giving us an income of twenty-five dollars a month. Unreal as it may seem, it kept us from going hungry and also kept our father, plus many others, from being counted among the unemployed, of which there soon would be millions all over the United States. By early 1933, one-fourth of the country's workers were without jobs. This meant that about fourteen million were unemployed. When the families were included, the number of Americans without a dependable source of income by early 1933 reached at least forty million. But on the Iron Range seventy percent of the workers were jobless.

Our mother began to take in sewing for the neighbors, but she charged so little for her work that it hardly paid her to do it. Unknowingly, she demeaned the value of her own labor. Most housewives I knew placed no value on their time and their work. They looked upon themselves as the servants of the family. Our mother sewed clothes for Rosemary Tisel, a Catholic neighbor's daughter, who was leaving home at the age of fourteen to prepare herself to become a nun. Rosemary already knew what she wanted to do with her life, even against her parents' wishes. How her mother wept the day she came to make arrangements for sewing Rosemary's clothes for her trip to the convent in Duluth! Irma and I sewed some of our own clothes, with our mother's help. We both babysat a half-block away for the Tingstad's son, Clifford, and his wife. Clifford was one of the fortunate ones; he had a steady job with the post office. For fifteen cents an hour, we put two children to bed, washed a big pile of dishes, pots and pans, and put the kitchen in order. Then we sat, often until one in the morning, sometimes earning as much as seventy-five cents a night.

To cut expenses, we had the telephone taken out. We ate a lot of spaghetti, macaroni, bread, and hamburger, all of which we liked, for Lempi was a good cook and the food was tasty. We had a big garden. The cost of food was reasonable. One dollar bought a lot of groceries. A 1930 ad from a newspaper listed: "A large 12-quart basket of extra fancy large Michigan Concord grapes, 33 cents. A bushel of Michigan Kiefer pears, 99 cents; 6 pounds of U.S. No. 1 Wealthy apples, 25 cents; a bushel, $1.49; a large white head of cauliflower, 10 cents; homemade assortment of cookies, one pound, 10 cents; American loaf cheese, one pound, 19 cents; mild Wisconsin or brick cheese, 2 pounds, 29 cents; fancy light meat tuna fish, one-half pound cans, 2 for 25 cents; fancy red Alaska salmon, No. 1 tall can, 15 cents; Goblin "All-Purpose" flour, 49-pound bag, 89 cents." Yes, a dollar could buy a lot of food, *if* you had the dollar.

The 1933 Sears Roebuck Christmas Catalogue listed a teddy bear at 59 cents; an alarm clock, 98 cents; four pounds of mixed nuts, 79 cents; and for 33 cents you could get a box of 25 Christmas cards with envelopes.

My brother Jorma tramped through the woods north of Virginia and shot an occasional rabbit, but we became concerned about tularemia, the rabbit disease, so we soon quit having wild rabbit on the menu. We ate a lot of fish that we caught in Vermilion and Burntside Lakes. We had a big garden, at first a plot provided by the school district on what we called the school farm, within walking distance just west of our house. Later we had a larger plot in the Oliver's large garden space for employees, called, naturally, the Oliver Gardens. The Oliver encouraged large gardens among its employees. Our whole family worked in the garden, where we planted potatoes, carrots, beets, and tomatoes.

Since our roomers all disappeared when there no longer was work for them in the mines or the sawmills, we rented an upstairs apartment to a newly married couple, Wilhart and Anna Nelson, children of Finnish immigrants from the nearby farming community of Cherry (*Alavus*). They paid a few dollars a month for three of the upstairs rooms. The fourth room we kept as a sleeping room for Jorma.

Now we could no longer make our monthly house payments to the former owner, John Kainula, who held our mortgage. He came to our house from time to time for the money, but there simply was nothing to give. We had already paid him almost $6,000 but still owed him $1194.33. We were now faced with the loss of our house. We shuddered at those terrible words, "foreclosing on your mortgage." Even we children feared what the loss of our house could mean to us as a family, for it was not only a house to us but the very center of our lives. We spent most of our time in it; we worked there together; our friends visited us there; it was our security base, the haven to which we children came at the end of the school day, to which our father came from the mine for rest and sustenance.

Somehow Otto and Lempi learned about the Home Owners' Loan Corporation (HOLC), which the new president, Franklin Delano Roosevelt, initiated in 1933 to lend homeowners money on long-term mortgages so they wouldn't lose their houses. On August 21, 1934, the federal government in the form of the HOLC paid Mr. Kainula the mortgage money due, $1194.33, and we began to pay the government $9.44 a month on the mortgage; the interest was five percent. Once each month our mother walked the mile and a half to the downtown post office to send a money order to the government, to Omaha, Nebraska, the regional office of the HOLC. Making that monthly payment became almost a ritual in our family. I have since learned that one-million homeowners were able to save their houses under this program, which did not end until 1951, but by 1932, 275,000 families had been evicted from their homes, before the Home Owners' Loan Corporation came to the rescue. By 1938, over 100,000 HOLC mortgages had been foreclosed. People simply could not pay even the HOLC mortgage. I do not know whether my parents, who had always voted the Republican ticket, voted for Mr. Roosevelt in 1936 for his second term, but I would hope they did.

The general custom was to charge the family's groceries at the neighborhood store and to pay the bill once a month. Even through the Depression years, we managed to do this—that is, to pay the bill each month and not to accumulate a large grocery debt. However, many families on the Range could not pay their grocery bills, or perhaps they preferred to, or had to, use their scarce money for other things. Some families owed the neighborhood grocers hundreds of dollars, at least this is what we heard. When a neighborhood grocer closed his store after the advent of a competing supermarket, he often went down with huge debts incurred by customers during the Depression, debts that probably were never paid.

During the Depression we could have been considered poor, but we never felt "poor." We were never hungry. We had the family, we had friends, the Church, the Temperance Society, the schools, and, of course, a good place to live, precarious as it may have been for a while. It wasn't until Mr. Kainmula began coming for his mortgage money that we realized just *how* precarious. Most of our neighbors and friends were in the same straits. The only financially secure families seemed to be the ones where the father worked for the school district (usually as a janitor), for the city, or for the post office. When their children graduated from high school, these parents were able to give them watches as graduation presents. For years, a wrist watch, the first one, was a standard high school graduation gift from parents. We were happy to be able to buy the five-dollar gold senior class ring.

Although we had a second-hand car, we did not use it very often now. Our father walked to work; it would not be until many years later that he would afford himself the luxury of driving to work. We walked everywhere, except to school. Junior and senior high school students, and also the junior college students, were picked up in the morning and returned home after school by an elaborate school bussing system. We might walk the one and a quarter miles home for noon lunch and back to school for the afternoon sessions, but mornings and afternoons we were delivered in style in fine busses. If at other times you simply had to ride the local bus, it cost a nickel to any place in the city. But usually we walked everywhere, for Virginia was not a large city.

Not only was the Depression plaguing the whole country, but the United States was suffering from a serious drought as well. From 1930 through 1935 a lack of rainfall devastated the Great Plains region and a huge dust bowl developed to cover about fifty-million acres. Although we were not physically a part of the Dust Bowl, as it came to be called, we were acutely aware of it through the newspapers, newsreels, radio, and discussions. Streams of farmers abandoned their drought-stricken farms and many headed west to California. Some families from Oklahoma and Texas walked all the way to California, the land of milk and honey. Most would never return to the lands they had left. Hall County, Texas, dropped from 40,000 population to 40. Farmers sold their sour cream for nine cents a pound and their eggs for ten cents a dozen.

We read about soup lines and bread lines. We didn't see them, but we did see the unemployed men huddled in the flimsy wood and tin Hoover camp shacks on the outskirts of Virginia, not far from our house—camps named for Herbert Hoover, president when the crash came in 1929. The Depression continued to worsen when he left the presidency in 1933.

It seemed as if the Depression lasted such a long time for us, from the end of 1929 until well into the 1940s. For so long the future looked dim. Our view of the world of opportunity was depressed; our sense of challenge was suppressed. Apathy and gloom lay over our lives. It covered the whole land; we were without hope. We felt as Oscar Wilde did when he wrote in his *Ballad of Reading Gaol:*

> *"Something was dead in each of us,*
> *And what was dead was hope."*

It seemed as if our family's life would be an endless struggle just to get along without overwhelming debts. Our family's confidence had disappeared. We simply no longer had a long-range view of where we were heading as a family or as individuals. Besides, we felt that our family had little or no effect on whatever future might lie ahead of us. There simply seemed to be nothing to look forward to.

In 1934 Otto did some "politicking" among the Finnish people for a candidate for county commissioner. His candidate won and Irma got work in the County Courthouse in Virginia, but only after our father strongly reminded the successful candidate of his promise for work. With her first paycheck, Irma bought a radio for the family, a lovely, large, wooden cabinet radio which took a place of honor on the west wall of the front room beside our father's favorite velour chair. For a long time both Irma and I had been embarrassed, also ashamed, because we had no radio. At school, when others talked about radio programs such as "Fibber McGee and Molly" or "Edgar Bergen and Charlie McCarthy," we remained silent, never admitting that we had no radio and had not heard the programs. But now we had a radio. We enjoyed it and our parents particularly enjoyed the Finnish programs broadcast from the Hibbing station.

President Roosevelt's various attempts to alleviate the Depression and the problems caused by the drought helped many of us, but as much as anything, he gave us the feeling that we could look to him for leadership. Through his "fireside chats" over the radio, through the newspapers and the newsreels, he made his presence known. We felt he was "in charge." He seemed like a personal friend and protector. Perhaps he helped to give us confidence in ourselves and our future, which still seemed so bleak. Yet it is my understanding that the United States did not really recover from the Great Depression that began in 1929 until the government began to spend heavily for defense in the 1940s.

Otto and we children dismantled the old sauna building board by board. Using many of the old boards, Otto constructed a fine two-car garage at the back of our lot, one stall of which was rented out for five dollars a month, free and clear. He built and painted white a backyard picket fence, planting lilacs for a privacy screen from the city sidewalk. Where the old public sauna had stood, he developed a lawn and a vegetable and flower garden. In their later years, Otto and Lempi were to enjoy this back yard, and they held many coffee parties and picnics there. Again, using boards from the old sauna, he designed and built a family sauna in the basement of our house, adding a modern touch, a shower.

For some years during the Depression and during our adolescent years, when we could not rent them out as no one had the cash money for rent, we used the four rooms upstairs as bedrooms for the family. Our parents had one room, our brother Jorma had another. Irma, Betty, and I took turns with the other two rooms, each of us getting a "room of her own" for part of each year. When Irma and I left home, three of the rooms upstairs were again rented to a young family, but with Jorma still retaining his room. Many years later, the upstairs was completely remodeled and rented out as a modern apartment.

In 1932, after graduating from high school, Irma got a summer job doing housework five days a week from nine in the morning until one in the afternoon, earning one dollar and fifty cents per week. Shortly afterward, she got a full-time housework job on the South Side at three dollars a week. Her salary was doubled, but so was her workday. I inherited her old part-time job working in the Oliver Location near us for an Oliver chemist, his wife, and one son. The work was easy—dusting, mopping, some light cooking, hanging out the wash in the back yard on Monday mornings, setting the table for lunch, washing the dishes afterward. I was never asked to do any of the heavy work. My employers were kind people. After a light lunch with the family, I did the dishes and walked home. I hope I did a good job, but doing housework held very little interest for me. I often ran the dry mop over the floor twice just to be sure I did a good job. I considered myself lucky to earn one dollar and fifty cents a week. It bought many things.

In the fall of 1932, after graduating from high school in June, Irma enrolled in the Virginia Junior College. I would do the same in 1933 after my high school graduation.

Trying to recall what the Depression meant, I realize that one can get by with very little in terms of the physical comforts money can buy, but cannot get along without support from the family, from friends and neighbors, and from the organizations and institutions one belongs to. With such a network of support, one *can* manage even in difficult times.

Looking back at the Depression and its long-time influence on my life and, later, my husband's life (his farm family in Nebraska suffered through the drought years as well as the Depression), I recognize that it has made both my husband and me overly careful and thrifty about money matters, which has sometimes worked to our disadvantage—like not putting a basement under a house we later built in Kentucky because it cost $1,200; many times we rued this "thrifty" decision. We carry as little debt as possible, although we recognize that sometimes it is wise to use credit, but at other times, its use can prove foolhardy. Living through the Depression influenced our lives forever.

Newspapers, Books, Phones

In our home in Virginia we received the *Virginia Daily Enterprise,* which eventually became the *Mesabi Daily News,* with my mother reading it more thoroughly than my father. After a day of working in the mine, plus his home chores, he often fell asleep reading the evening paper. Occasionally, during the Depression, one of us children would walk down to St. Denis's Green Store at Ninth Street North and Sixth Avenue to pick up a Sunday edition of the *Duluth News Tribune.* When the Depression began to ease, we ordered the daily *Duluth News Tribune* and its Sunday edition, plus the *Range Facts,* a weekly paper published in Virginia and distributed over the Range. We children looked forward to reading the Range news each week in the newspaper.

Six days a week, we got the Finnish *Päivälehti* (Daily News), published in Duluth. The paper covered world, United States, state, and local news, and seemed a neutral paper which did not promote any special points of view. It ceased publication in 1948. We also subscribed to the *Minnesotan Uutiset* (Minnesota News) published three times a week in New York Mills, Minnesota, by the Parta Printers, Inc. In 1960 *Minnesotan Uutiset* became the *Amerikan Uutiset* (American News), enlarging its news coverage. For many years it was published every Thursday. In 1984 the paper was moved to Lantana, Florida, where many Finns from both the United States and Finland live. The paper advertised itself as "The Voice of Finland in America." We children seldom read the Finnish-American papers, but from time to time Lempi read articles out loud to us. She was an unusually able reader, considering that she had gone to school for only four years. Every day she read newspapers, magazines, books, most of them in Finnish. From my childhood on, I considered her an intelligent, articulate woman, but only in our Finnish world, of course.

One Finnish newspaper that we did not get but saw often in the homes of friends and neighbors was the *Työmies* (The Working Man). First published in Hancock, Michigan, as a voice for Finnish copper miners, it was moved in 1914 to Superior, Wisconsin, where it is being published today as *Työmies-Eteenpäin* (The Working Man-Forward). The paper is generally Socialist-oriented and written from the perspective of working class people.

We also occasionally saw, in some homes, a newspaper called the *Industrialisti* (The Industrialist). This was published weekly by the I.W.W. (The Industrial Workers of the World) to which many Finnish workers belonged.

Every year we also bought the Finnish annuals published in the United States. For many years these were hard-cover books. Later they were also available in paperback. They were called *kalenterit* (calendars) and included the *Raittiuskansan kalenteri* (The Temperance People's Calendar), first published in 1896; the *Kirkollinen kalenteri* (The Church Calendar), begun in 1903; and the *Siirtokansan kalenteri* (The Immigrants' Calendar) originating in 1918. All of them had calendars in the first part of the book, giving not only the days of the year but also name days *(nimipäivät)*, which were of great significance to the Finns from the Old Country. These names were people's given, or first, names and every day in the year had a designated name or names assigned to it. These name days seemed more important than birthdays. Even today, the weekly *Amerikan Uutiset* newspaper lists Finnish name days. For example, one issue listed these name days: Thursday, Valto, Valdemar; Friday, Pälvi, Pilvi; Saturday, Lauha; Sunday, Anssi; Monday, Alina; Tuesday, Yrjö, Jyrki, Yrjäna, Jyri, Jori; Wednesday, Pertti, Albert, Altti.

The *Immigrants' Calendar,* or *Annual,* perhaps the most popular of the three books and certainly the one we children were most interested in, listed the American and Finnish holidays for each month, plus other important days to note, such as: "February 28, 1835, Kalevala Day. First publication of the *Kalevala.*"

The first pages of the *Immigrants' Calendar* also included geographical and governmental information about the United States, information about its flag, the Pledge of Allegiance, the Star Spangled Banner, the President and his Cabinet, the weights and measures used in this country, plus other information that could be of value to immigrants, particularly information about laws that affected them. Printed in their own language, the *Immigrants' Calendar* helped to educate the Finns about their new country, and taught them the obligations and privileges of citizenship. All three books kept them in touch with the Old Country and also with Finns all over the United States. They served as vehicles to Americanize the Finns, and they also served as networks to maintain the Finnish language and culture in the United States. They contained articles, stories, and original poetry written by the immigrants.

The *Church Calendar* concerned itself primarily with religious matters and the *Temperance Calendar* with temperance matters. All the books contained pictures and life stories of well-known Finns, plus prominent Americans. They also included many group pictures of the Finnish organizations in this country. The *Immigrants' Calendar* featured pictures and articles of immigrant children who had succeeded in some field. This was particularly true during World War II. The last section of the books was given to death notices of immigrants and their children who had died during the past year *(Vainajien muistolle)*, with pictures and stories of their lives.

These annuals were a great way for Finns all over the United States to keep in touch with each other, for in the early years we had no telephones or radios, only letters, newspapers, and books. We children paged through these annuals interested mostly in the pictures, which were often of people and places we knew.

Today, four weekly Finnish newspapers continue to be published in the United States: *New Yorkin Uutiset* (New York News) in Brooklyn, New York; *Amerikan Uutiset* (American News) in Lantana, Florida; *Raivaaja* (The Pioneer) in Fitchburg, Massachusetts, and *Työmies-Eteenpäin* (The Working Man-Forward) in Superior, Wisconsin.

When our family moved to Virginia, we had a telephone for the first time. In the beginning, it seldom rang, for it took time to make new friends; besides, not many of our newly acquired friends had telephones in 1925. But as more and more Finns got telephones, our telephone got more and more use. At first, our mother was timid, actually afraid, to answer the telephone for fear that it might be a *toiskielinen* (someone who did not speak Finnish), and she would not be able to understand what was said. So in the early years, we children usually answered the telephone. Making calls on the telephone also presented problems, since the caller had to give the desired number to the operator. So here again our mother had qualms about being able to pronounce the telephone numbers well enough to be understood by the operator, so at first we children gave the operator the number. During the Depression we had no money for such a luxury as a telephone, and it was taken out. By the time it was reinstated a number of years later, our mother's trepidation about using the telephone had pretty much dissipated. Most of the calls were for her. She also made many calls, for the coming of the dial telephone eliminated the need to speak with the operator. I do not remember ever seeing our father use the telephone. And, of course, casual long-distance calls were simply unheard of. Only in matters of serious illness or death were long distance calls resorted to. So for many years a long-distance call was one to be answered with considerable trepidation, fear, and alarm.

This drawing by Diane Heusinkveld of the birchbark shoes sent to the Väänänen family from Finland serves as a cover illustration for Inkeri Väänänen-Jensen's translation of "Forbidden Fruit and Other Tales by Juhani Aho."

Early Links
to Finland

There was no place to go but up, American style, or so most of us thought. Both of our parents seemed to feel that they would never return to Finland. After many years of laboring with low pay, with four children to support, a house to pay for, all compounded by the many years of the Depression during what should have been their most productive years, our parents had no extra money for such a trip. At least in my childhood, returning to Finland, even for a visit, was never mentoned. As far as I could tell, it was never even a remote possibility. Yet, to my surprise, I did discover a passport application to visit his mother that my father had filled out in 1920. For some reason, such a trip never materialized, and I can only surmise that the money simply was not available. This aborted trip was never mentioned within the family.

Through the years, Lempi wrote regularly to Finland, primarily to her sisters, Tyyne Mäkinen and Martha Lehtonen, and when they had passed on, to their daughters, my cousins, particularly Salli Pentinsaari, Aino Tanner, and Aili Uusiniemi. They exchanged many pictures so we got to know my mother's family quite well through them, as well as through the letters. As teenagers, Irma and I wrote to our cousins, Aino and Aili, but our Finnish was too "American." We learned that they laughed heartily at our writing attempts, which quickly put an end to those attempts. We actually didn't realize that we were writing American-type Finnish, using American words with Finnish endings tacked on; nor did we know that there is a considerable difference between spoken Finnish and written, or literary, Finnish. We were innocently writing our spoken, American-type Finnish, now called "Finglish."

Occasionally, Lempi wrote to her father and I remember her crying when, in 1921, she got word that he had died. We, his American grandchildren, felt bad that our mother was crying, but we did not have a feeling of personal loss.

Through letters and pictures from our mother's and father's families and the magazines we got from Finland, we also got to know and share in the travail, in the struggle for the basic needs in food and clothing of the Finnish people during their 1939-1940 Winter War with Russia, and the later difficult aftermath of World War II, in which the Finns had sided with Germany against their common Russian enemy.

In immigrant families, the letter writing was done mostly by the wife and mother. Lempi, instead of Otto, wrote to his family in Finland, even though she had never met any of them except—briefly in Ely—Joope Väänänen and Emil Vänninen in the early 1920s. Our Väänänen relatives also sent pictures, but we did not feel as close to them as we did to our mother's family. After Finland's Winter War with Russia and World War II, we sent clothing, coffee, money, and many, many CARE packages to both the Helander and Väänänen sides of the family, more to our mother's family as most of her relatives had become city people while Otto's were still mainly on their farms and could manage better in getting life's basic necessities. In return, through the years, our relatives sent us gifts, mostly gifts of art—huge ceramic plates, designer glassware, handwoven tablecloths, runners, jewelry (much of it made from wood), wall hangings of many kinds, birchbark baskets, birchbark shoes. We exhibited these gifts with great pride to our friends, neighbors, and visitors. It was as if we ourselves gained in stature through the quality of these gifts. We borrowed from their talent to give ourselves a prestige that seemed somehow lacking in our own lives as members of an immigrant family in America.

We basked in reflected glory over the success of Paavo Nurmi, the great Olympic running star of the 1920s. We were proud of Jean Sibelius, the Finnish composer, and the architects, Eliel and Eero Saarinen, Alvar Aalto. We were proud of the textile designs of Marimekko, the pottery of Arabia. But our life centered around our Finnish environment in America. Finland was a faraway foreign country, at least to us children. Even our close relatives in Finland seemed unreal in the sense that they were thousands of miles away, and there was no way that we would ever see them. Our closest contact would always be only through letters and pictures.

ollege, University

In the fall of 1933, after having been graduated from Virginia's Roosevelt High School in June, I stepped across the street, back to the old Virginia Technical High School, which I had first entered as a seventh grader six years earlier, and enrolled now as a freshman in the Virginia Junior College in the east end of the building. It was the heart of the Depression; there were few jobs, so the largest percentage of our graduating class went on to school, most of us to the junior college across the street.

The tuition was five dollars a semester, ten dollars for the year. There was a small locker fee (refunded at the end of the year), and minor laboratory fees. Books were reasonably priced in the college bookstore and could usually be sold back to the store, if necessary. Students came in from nearby towns, from Mt. Iron, Kinney, Buhl, Gilbert. Many of them were Finns, with names like Junnila, Kauppila, Koskela, Laine, Leinonen, Metsa, Neittamo, Niskanen, Tuomi, Vanhala. We Finns may have had the most trouble with our names— in pronunciation, I mean—but the Slovenians and Italians also had their troubles. In junior college I remember particularly one girl from Kinney, Vukasava Lumovich, whose parents were Serbian, specifically from Montenegro. Because of her name, Vukie, as we affectionately called her, always stood out from the crowd during roll calls. Vukie had a refreshing, naive spirit, with a natural skill for storytelling—in which she engaged to the delight of the women students as we relaxed in the women's social room. Most of Vukie's stories revolved about the customs of Montenegrin peasants, still observed in her home, which particularly impressed the "American" girls, whose home life was so different from that of the Slav peasant transplanted into America in the first decades of the 1900s.

The school boards in the neighboring Range towns provided transportation to Virginia for their junior college students, either by running a school bus to Virginia or by donating money for carpooling if there were not enough students for a busload. Because costs at this time were minimal, a pattern developed whereby students came to Virginia, even from other states. They stayed with relatives or friends, or rented apartments or houses, sometimes four to six in a house. They chose Virginia Junior College for its low tuition fee of ten dollars a year, its excellent teachers, its offerings in varied fields of study, and its many opportunities in drama, debate, athletics, journalism, music, and art. Eventually, "outsiders" began to pay higher fees than those living within the junior college district.

About two blocks from the Technical High School, in which the junior college was located, was the college hangout, Bye's Bakery, where for fifteen cents you could get a cup of coffee and a Napoleon, a wonderfully light, French puff pastry with a delicious custard filling. Doughnuts, cookies, rolls were also available, but it was the Napoleon that was the peak of Bye's Bakery's artistry and skill for most of us. But, sadly, it was not very often that we had the fifteen cents to stop in at Bye's as most of us were operating on a no-cash basis. Many of us managed to lunch for two cents a day from the penny line in the school cafeteria shared by junior high, senior high, junior college students, and teachers, where for a penny we could buy a large bowl of soup or a large cup of cocoa with crackers. With another penny's worth of crackers, we enjoyed what we looked upon as our "Depression lunch."

One pleasant social event of the junior college years was the annual pasty supper held in the women's city clubrooms for the women students of the college. The pasty, meat and potatoes in a crust, was a popular food on the Range, and we all looked forward to this event.

While in junior college, I worked part-time as the bookkeeper and general salesgirl in a women's ready-to-wear store on Main Street. Our family had been buying women's shoes, hose, dresses, coats, and hats there for many years, and I was happy to be offered the job. My take-home pay averaged eighteen cents an hour. By 1938 the minimum hourly wage would zoom to twenty-five cents. This, however, was 1933. Part of my work as bookkeeper was to send out dunning letters to customers who were neglecting to pay their bills. I was surprised to discover to whom the letters were sent, to people I had looked upon as well-to-do and responsible. None of them were Finns, I was happy to note.

A custom had developed in this and in some other stores, that when purchasing larger items like coats and dresses, the buyer would try to get the price lowered from the ticket price on the garment. The clerk would call the owner or manager to look at the coat or dress in question, and the buyer would make an offer of less than the listed price. After some haggling, a price, lower than the marked price, but usually higher than what the buyer wanted to pay, would be agreed upon, and the sale was made.

I was enrolled as a physical education major, with the intent to teach, teaching at this time being the most popular field selected by Rangers who planned to finish college. The junior college had many able teachers and interesting classes and generally, the years spent there were satisfying ones for most of us. It was a safe, friendly place of some four-hundred students, and we were learning to look at the world with a broader view than we had previously. I remember particularly the excellent plays the students put on under the able direction of Mary E. Asseltyne, teacher of speech and also the drama coach. In the play "Big-Hearted Herbert," I had the good fortune to take the role of a young boy. The play was one of high humor and sometimes during the rehearsals the cast would be so convulsed with laughter that we were unable to carry on. It was a joyous, high-spirited experience. I have the feeling that high school and college students who were in plays remember them with fondness and nostalgia.

I finished junior college in June, 1935, but since there were no full-time jobs available, nor money for going away to college, I spent another year in J.C., as we called it, taking business courses—typing, shorthand, accounting—training to become a secretary. I continued working at The Minnesota Store. It was then that I got my social security number, for in 1935 the Social Security Act was passed as part of President Roosevelt's New Deal program.

In the fall of 1936, I entered the University of Minnesota in Minneapolis as a junior in the social work department. I had changed my major from physical education to social work; I don't really remember why. I received a National Youth Administration (NYA) grant, and worked in the social work offices for a monthly stipend of twenty dollars. The NYA, established in 1935, was a part of the WPA, the Works Progress Administration of President Roosevelt's New Deal. Without this help, I probably would not have reached the University. My sister Irma, who was now working in the County Courthouse in Duluth, and later, my brother Jorma, who began working in the same mine as our father, both sent me money each month. The costs, including tuition ($13.25 per quarter in the

College of Science, Literature, and the Arts), books, food, housing, all travel, some clothing (one year even included a winter coat), for the nine-month school year was five-hundred dollars.

The University students from the Iron Range had organized a Rangers' Club, meeting once a month for social activities and also for chartering busses for trips back to the Range at vacation times. The cost was five dollars for a round trip to most Range towns. I served one year as secretary of the Rangers' Club. Our favorite songs were the Slovenian *"Moya Dekla"* (My Girl) and the western "Home on the Range." In fact, I believe they were the only songs we sang, but we sang them with sentiment and gusto. Belonging to the Rangers' Club gave many of us the psychological support of "hometown folks" that a number of us needed in the big, impersonal University.

During the 1930s, "batching" was one way of economizing one's way through college. Many of the owners of large old houses ringing the University rented rooms with kitchen privileges. I stayed at a house with nine other University women, two to a room, each woman with a single bed. Most of the basement was given over to a cooking and eating area, our place of "batching." Since there were corner groceries nearby, and we were also close to the University business section known as Dinkytown, purchasing food to cook was no problem and usually the store was on the way home from classes. To celebrate after an exam, or for a break from cooking on Sunday, we would splurge and go out to eat an evening or a Sunday dinner to enjoy soup or juice, a salad, meat, potatoes, another vegetable, rolls, a drink, and dessert, often pie—for thirty-five cents. I do not believe we ever left a tip. We were lucky to have the thirty-five cents to cover the cost of the meal. Our favorite spot was just off the campus on University Avenue near the old Perine's Bookstore—both places long since demolished from those sites. The ten of us in the house became friends, helped each other when necessary, gathering often in the evenings in each other's rooms for long discussions.

Of the ten women in the house, only one other was a Finn, Verna Koskela of Keewatin, a Range town. Her parents had a successful grocery store there and also "ran" a boardinghouse. Verna's two brothers, Lauri and Albert, were in medical school at the University and both became doctors.

At home we had not used cuss words or sworn in either Finnish or English. Swearing was not a pattern in our family life, nor among our friends. We knew, of course, that *saatana* (Satan) and *perkele*

(Devil) were the most violent of Finnish swear words, but we did not use them at home. When these two words are pronounced with vigor, strongly accented on the first syllable, they sound appropriately vehement and downright vulgar. However, upon reaching the University, I threw caution to the winds and became, at least for a while, a reckless user of "damn" and "hell." This I considered most daring—in 1935.

I was twenty years old and had never tasted beer. At the University, the nearby beer taverns were popular night spots and hangouts for students. The several times I went to one of these taverns, I tried hard to drink the beer, but usually ended up eating the popcorn and pretzels and drinking as little beer as possible. The taverns simply did not interest me as a place to hang out.

After one quarter in the Social Work Department, I transferred to the College of Education to train to become a high school English and Social Studies teacher, slipping into the field being pursued by most students from the Range, at least those I knew. I had discovered that there was no hope of getting a job in social work without a master's degree, and I could not see how I could afford to spend three years at the University. Getting a paying job as soon as possible was of utmost importance to a child of the Depression. Teaching, I hoped, would offer economic security as quickly as any other field of work. I also felt I could develop into a good teacher.

From the two years I spent at the University, I remember two outstanding teachers: Dr. Asher Christensen in political science and Dr. Horace T. Morse in education. Dr. Christensen was an exciting, brilliant lecturer. There were five hundred in the political science class so I never knew him personally, but his well-organized, dynamic, yet scholarly lectures were impressive. In the final exam, I believe I got the highest grade in the class. I considered myself a serious student. Dr. Morse was a particularly well-prepared, scholarly, kind teacher of future teachers. Unfortunately, both men died too early in their careers, depriving many students of excellent teaching. Generally speaking, I was not impressed by the teaching in the classes I had at the University. I felt that the teachers in the Virginia high school and junior college were more skillful in the "art" of teaching. Maybe it was because we were individuals to them, not just one of a vast number on a large university campus.

In June 1938, I was one of 1,800 graduating from the University of Minnesota. I was graduated "with distinction" with an education

Graduation,
University of Minnesota

major in English, a minor in Social Studies.

I spent the summer of 1938 applying for teaching jobs in a number of small towns in Minnesota. Teaching jobs were hard to find; the Depression was still keeping a lid on opportunities to work. In order to help the fledgling teachers from their towns, some school boards on the Range had instituted a system of "cadet" teachers. For a hundred dollars a month, unemployed and new teachers were hired to assist regular teachers. This was a great boon for many young education graduates, of whom the Range had so many. This "cadet" system had ended, at least in Virginia, by 1938, or at least I do not remember applying for a job as a "cadet" teacher, or even realizing that it was available as an option. Fortunately, in the waning weeks of that summer, I *did* get a teaching job.

A Short Teaching Career

In 1938 I was hired as the librarian, also teaching English and Business, at Askov, Minnesota, for $100 a month or $900 for the nine-month school year. Askov was a village of 300 in eastern Minnesota on Highway 23 just east of Interstate 35. It had been settled by Danish immigrants. The major farm crop was rutabagas. The school was consolidated, meaning that most of the students were bussed in from the surrounding rural area. The one-room schoolhouse out in the country had disappeared. I did not know it, but taking the job at Askov was to change the course of my life.

The teaching and administrative staff at Askov consisted of ten people, of which four were of Danish background. One of the "American" men teachers was married to a Dane, and the one "American" woman teacher eventually married one of Askov's Danish farmers. One teacher was an Irish Catholic, another was of Norwegian descent, another of Swedish ancestry, and I was Finnish. Chris Jensen and his wife, the custodians who kept the school shipshape, were both Danish immigrants. Most of the pupils, about 110 in junior and senior high and 120 in the elementary grades, had Danish backgrounds. The most common last names among the students were Andersen, Hansen, Jacobsen, Jensen, Johnsen, Olesen, Olsen, Petersen, all with the Danish *"-sen"* ending. I was not used to the cultural homogeneity that I met here; the polyglot Iron Range consisted of forty-three different nationalities.

The Askov school had a remarkable Danish library, separate from the regular school library. This was the first school I had encountered in which the predominant local foreign language was acually taught in the public school, the name of which, by the way, was the H. C. Andersen School. In many homes on the Iron Range, a language other than English was the primary language, and in the schools, only the "standard" high school foreign languages—Latin, French, and German—were taught. It never entered our minds to ask that Finnish or any language of the immigrants be studied within the school system. That was simply unthinkable! Of what value were they? We had learned that the language we spoke at home had no value. Many of us were ashamed of our native language, ashamed that English was not the language spoken at home, ashamed of our parents' fragmented, "broken" English. This was a time in American history when it seemed an advantage to speak and know only one language—English. So it was surprising and refreshing to come to Askov to find strong Danish language classes and a Danish library as integral parts of the school.

I had considerable adjusting to do, however, because almost all the students were of Danish background. Many of them were related to each other, and all of them were friends, or so it seemed. The school was almost like one big, friendly, chattering family which gathered together every school day to continue their socializing.

On the Range and at the University, I had been used to large school buildings with wide halls, marble floors, hundreds of students, but very little noise. In Askov, the small, red brick H. C. Andersen School in which all the pupils, grades one through twelve, were housed, seemed like bedlam when the students clattered noisily between classes along the wooden floors and up and down the wooden stairs, chatting and laughing as they moved. The general atmosphere of the school was relaxed and there were many able students. Askov itself proved to be a friendly village. The teachers were invited into many homes, and the first year passed quickly.

One teacher with a Danish background, Harald Jensen, from the Danish pioneer village of Nysted, Nebraska, named after a town in Denmark, taught social studies and biology, and was in charge of boys' athletics, with boys' basketball as the primary school sport. He coached the most successful basketball team in the school's history, winning the district title and moving into the regional playoffs.

The supportive community, in busses and cars, followed their victorious team to their out-of-town games, and we sang the school song with gusto, both on the bus and at the games:

> *"We feed our boys on rutabagas,*
> *Rutabagas, rutabagas,*
> *We feed our boys on rutabagas,*
> *So they'll grow big and strong!"*

Askov was known as "The Rutabaga Capital of the World."

Because of his Danish background, Harald knew some of the

136

Askov people through the nationwide Danish church and its young people's groups. One day, his friends, Ed and Wilda Rix, who were from Tyler, Minnesota, another Danish community, suggested he invite one of the women teachers to join him to play bridge at their house. He walked over to the house where Solveig Utoft, who taught the Danish language classes and also Danish gymnastics for the girls, lived, to invite her, but she was not at home. So as a second choice, he invited me. I *was* at home. I have forgotten that particular evening, except that I did not know very much about playing bridge, but from then on, Harald's and my friendship began to develop. We began to go to the movies in the nearby towns of Sandstone and Moose Lake, usually with friends as neither Harald nor I had a car.

When Solveig Utoft left Askov the next year to teach in a Wisconsin school, Helga Miller from Pine City drove up each day to continue the Danish language classes, and I took over the girls' gymnastics, in which we followed the gymnastics system developed in Denmark by Niels Bukh. I have since learned that the Danish language was taught in the Askov school until 1943.

During my second year of teaching, Harald bought a blue, second-hand Chevrolet coupe, which the students dubbed "The Blue Goose." We drove to Duluth, some sixty miles away, to see that great epic of the South, "Gone with the Wind." For many young people, seeing a movie together was the most common kind of date, and so it was for Harald and me.

After two years of teaching and coaching at Askov, Harald moved to Tyler as junior high principal, also teaching English and physical education. I went to the small southern Minnesota community of Delavan as school principal, English teacher, and librarian. One had to be versatile to teach in the small town high schools of Minnesota.

Marriage and World War II

In September, 1941, Harald and I were married by the Reverend Victor Kuusisto of Virginia's Finnish Evangelical Lutheran Church in the living room of our home; only a small group was present.

After a honeymoon visit to Harald's relatives in Tyler and Nysted, Nebraska, we moved to Ames, Iowa, where Harald worked at Iowa State College (later University) toward his master's degree in agricultural economics. During the summer of 1941, I had attended the Duluth Business University to become more expert at typing and shorthand, which I had taken in junior college. At Ames, I began doing office and secretarial work at the College for thirty-five cents an hour. Some wives would later say that they earned a degree too, the Ph. T. degree, "Putting Hubby Through."

And now in Ames began the "shelving" of my Finnishness. As Ingrid Waananen in Minnesota there was no doubt who I was, but as Ingrid Jensen in Iowa, who was I? Nobody asked "What nationality are you?" "Jensen" was such an easy name to pronounce. It seldom elicited an inquiry as to its origin, for there were many Danes in Iowa.

In our two years in Ames, we often drove to Des Moines, only thirty miles away, where Harald's uncle, Alfred C. Nielsen, was Dean of Grand View College, a junior college established in 1896 by the Danish American Evangelical Lutheran Church. It was also the seminary for training ministers for the Danish church, much as Suomi College in Hancock, Michigan, was for the Finns.

Harald finished his master's degree at Iowa State in 1943. Drafted, he was sent to basic training at Camp Barkeley, Texas, and was trained as a clerk in the Medical Corps of the Army. In December I joined him and got a job as secretary to the office manager of the Swift and Company packing plant in Abilene, Texas. After basic training, Harald was assigned to Camp Polk, Louisiana, as a clerk in the Medical Corps; I worked as a clerk for the Quartermaster Corps there. Within a few months Harald entered officers' training at Carlisle Barracks, Pennsylvania. I now returned to Virginia as a pregnant army wife, to live once again with my parents. Our son

Rudolf was born May 19, 1945, delivered by "The Doctor," our old neighbor, J. Arnold Malmstrom.

The sudden death of President Roosevelt on April 12, 1945, shocked us and marred the joy of the end of the European war on May 5 and the war with Japan on August 14. Most of us did not know how the new president, Harry S. Truman, would measure up in his role as successor to the strong and dynamic President Roosevelt.

Yet it was a happy experience as Rudy and I stayed with my parents for the first seven months of his life. My parents were able to enjoy the presence of a grandchild without the responsibility for his care, and I, in turn, had considerable freedom to come and go during this interim period while we waited to join Harald, who had not been sent overseas. A number of my friends, also married to servicemen, had returned to the homes of their parents, especially if they had children or were pregnant. I was thus able to renew old friendships. Also, my sister Betty was in Virginia, living in an apartment with her three-year-old twin sons while her husband, Wilfred Parsinen, stationed in Alaska, repaired planes for the U.S. Air Force on the Adak Islands. As a Private, Harald's total pay was $50 a month, of which $28 plus an additional $22 contributed by the Army was sent to me and Rudy. I gave my parents $20 a month for the privilege of living with them.

In many ways, it was a woman's world with so many of them waiting for husbands to return, waiting for that future happy reunion. Besides being back with many women friends, I was also back in a Finnish area. We spoke Finnish at home or, I should say, the American-type Finnish we all, my parents included, had developed through the years. Once again I could enjoy a refreshing sauna in the basement. Many old Finnish friends, the Mäkis, Kemppis, Niskalas, Siirolas, Lehtos, came to visit on Wednesday and Saturday nights, sauna nights. After our saunas, we enjoyed coffee, often served with Finnish biscuit, the standard coffee bread in Finnish homes, and conversed in a mixture of Finnish and English. On occasion, we visited old friends in Ely, the Kivipeltos, the Maenpääs, the Porthans.

In December, 1945, Rudy and I were able to join Harald at Fitzsimmons General Hospital in Denver, Colorado, where, as a second lieutenant in the Medical Corps of the Army, he was serving as the assistant director of dietetics. One of his responsibilities was to go into the Denver markets once a week to purchase fresh fruits

Inkeri and Harald and their first born, Rudy,1945.

and vegetables for the hospital. We lived in officer quarters on the hospital grounds in huge rooms filled with dark, heavy, stark Army furniture. All the officers, mostly doctors and their wives, living in these quarters were "Americans." At least the subject of immigrant backgrounds was never raised. Our Danish and Finnish heritages were never mentioned. No one asked, "What nationality are you?"

In September 1946, our second son, Paul, was born in Denver. In November, Harald was discharged from the Army after three years of service. We had $1,000, two sons, and no job.

Iowa, Kentucky, Indiana, and A New Era in Minnesota

After celebrating Christmas with Harald's mother and other relatives in Nysted, Nebraska, we returned in January, 1947, to Ames and Iowa State, where Harald taught economics and studied for his Ph.D. in agricultural economics. We lived in student housing, army barracks built for the great influx of returning veterans and their families. They were small, but well-designed. We renewed our friendships among the Danes in Des Moines and enlarged our friendship circle in Ames.

Now that the war was over, many young couples were having their postponed children. It was a busy, happy life. Most of our friends were not sons and daughters of immigrants, or at least the matter never came up for discussion. The Iron Range and its close ties to many nationalities now seemed far away. Our life was an upwardly mobile one, although we were not really aware of this. The days were filled with hard work for both of us.

In 1950 Harald received his Ph.D. in agricultural economics, and we purchased our first house–in Ames. After three years of a comfortable middle class existence, we moved in 1953 to Lexington, Kentucky, where Harald became an associate professor in agricultural economics at the University of Kentucky. I became Sunday School superintendent and president of the Faith Lutheran Church Women, and Harald served as the adult Sunday School teacher. I was startled to see the president of the church women smoking while she conducted a meeting. This was not what I was used to in Midwest Lutheran Ladies' Aids! Anyhow, the women were a wonderful, liberal group to work with, and we had many fine times together. Our daughter, Katharine, was born in Lexington in 1957, and was baptized in Faith Church. In our four years in Kentucky, the only Finnish people we had any contact with were my Aunt Sylvia Salovaara from Cincinnati and her Finnish friends, Mr. and Mrs. Ala, who were employed on a horse farm just outside Lexington.

Nationalities were never discussed with our friends in Kentucky. Our name, Jensen, was an uncommon one here. From time to time we were called "Jenkins." More than once I was introduced as Ingrid Bergman, the only Ingrid with whom our Kentucky friends seemed familiar. I got the impression that they had little concept of the vast European migrations to the United States between 1880 and 1925 and their impact.

In 1957 we moved to West Lafayette, Indiana, where Harald became an associate professor at Purdue University. We lived in the heart of the city, with sidewalks, alleys, and the opportunity to walk to work and to shopping. We felt a freedom of movement that we had not felt in suburban living.

I became friends with Lillian Henriksen, who lived about a block away. Her husband was a Dane from New York City, now on the Purdue mathematics staff. With great amazement, I learned that Lillian was the daughter of our old Ely neighbors, the Santapakkas, who had changed their name to Hill. She had been Lillian Hill, born after we had moved from Ely.

We had barely settled down to a comfortable, small-town life when Harald was offered work as a full professor at the University of Minnesota on its St. Paul campus. In July, 1958, we moved to Minnesota.

During all those years away from Minnesota, we had used our summer vacations to visit our parents. Now it was easy for our mothers to visit us, and we made frequent visits to them. We spent our summer vacations at nearby lakes relaxing, swimming, boating, and fishing. In 1968, with two other families, we bought an old resort on Bluewater Lake near Grand Rapids in what we considered an idyllic northern Minnesota setting, with birches, evergreen forests, and a clear, blue lake with clean and sandy shores.

Although we were now back in the state with many Finns and descendants of Finns, we rarely saw any of them. Ted Salminen, who grew up in the rural Finnish community of Pike River, not too far from Virginia, lived across the street. My sister Irma and her husband, Henry Parsinen, with their five children, moved from Duluth to nearby Hopkins in 1959, and we visited each other from time to time. We did not speak Finnish except when Henry's parents, Hilda and Henry, or our mother came to visit, but we did enjoy telling and listening to Finnish-American jokes and stories. Our brother Jorma, a watchmaker in Duluth, had married Leona

Anderson, whose mother was Swedish and whose father was Norwegian. Leona and Jorma had four children. Whenever we got together, Jorma seemed to have a new supply of what we considered hilarious Finnish jokes—often jokes involving Finnish reactions to American life, which he told in a skillful, and what we considered a "true" Finnish accent.

We lived a comfortable, middle-class American suburban life in a friendly neighborhood. Our sons were busy with friends, Boy Scouts, school, and athletics. Our daughter was involved in school, dancing, piano lessons, and playing with her many friends in the neighborhood. Harald was fully occupied with teaching, research, and writing. We were active in St. Michael's Lutheran Church, at that time a part of the Swedish Augustana Synod. I was a suburban housewife, raising children, cleaning house, cooking, chauffeuring, shopping, doing a limited amount of volunteer work, reading a lot. Most of our friends were from the academic community on the St. Paul campus. As far as I could tell, few of them had recent immigrant backgrounds. If they did, these were never mentioned. We spoke only English in our home, but when my mother visited us, she and I would speak Finnish. When Harald's mother came, she often spoke with Harald in Danish, which remained her favored language. Our children were not interested in learning either of these two languages, nor did we even think about trying to teach them.

In all the years after I left home in 1935, I wrote every week, usually on Sunday, to my parents, and after my father died in 1949, to my mother. I always wrote in Finnish, or I should say in the American-style Finnish we immigrant children had learned. During most of these years, my mother also wrote to me every week. My last letter to her arrived after her death in 1974, and was returned to me. I did not have the courage to open it. Harald also wrote weekly to his mother—in Danish. But our children had no part in these two "immigrant" languages that, for Harald and me, were still such a large part of our inner lives. In school, our children's "important" languages were German, French, and Latin.

Visiting the Old Countries

It was a rare immigrant who could return to his or her native land. Some of us in the next generation would find it possible. We had occasionally talked about going out of the United States for a year. Harald was preparing for his sabbatical leave from the University. After some exchange of letters, it was arranged that he would lecture on agricultural economics in Denmark, Norway, Finland, Sweden, and Germany—in that order.

In 1964, arriving in Rotterdam on a Holland-America ship, we picked up a small Opel station wagon, the purchase of which we had arranged before leaving St. Paul. On October 1, again by prior arrangement, we left our sons at the *Snoghøj* (Snake Mound) Folk High School near the town of Fredericia in the Jutland Peninsula of Denmark. Rudy and Paul were to work on the school farm until school started in a month. Their boss, the farm manager, spoke no English, so their spoken language lessons began immediately. Harald, Kate, and I headed for Copenhagen, where Harald would lecture for three months at the Royal Agricultural College, and where we enrolled Kate in the public elementary *Ny Carlsbergvejens Skole* (New Carlsberg Street School) near Denmark's famous Carlsberg Brewery. She was seven years old. We learned that all her teachers spoke English. Soon she was making friends with her classmates and learning enough Danish to get along with them. Later we learned that from time to time she was asked to read in English for the upper grades where English was being taught. The teachers wanted their students to hear an American child read the English language. So now all our children were learning Danish. Harald remembered Danish from his childhood. Conducting his classes in Danish, he was often taken for a native of Denmark. When he said he was from the United States, the next question often was, "When, then, did you leave Denmark for the United States?"

We lived with Karen Brill, whose cousin we had known in Ames. We did much sightseeing, visiting museums, zoos, historic churches, castles, and ancient, out-of-the-way villages. We rode the big ferries and shopped on Copenhagen's *Strøget,* a long street banned to all car and truck traffic. We were invited into many friendly and charming homes. At Christmas our sons came down from their folk school, and we shared a traditional Danish Christmas with Karen Brill.

After Christmas our sons returned to their folk school, and Harald, Kate, and I drove to Ås, a tiny Norwegian village a few kilometers from Oslo, where we spent several weeks while Harald lectured in English to the Agricultural Economics and Rural Sociology faculty of Norway's College of Agriculture.

Here we were generously invited into Norwegian homes for festive dinners. Living in Ås were Lea and Arne Lokken, friends from our days at Iowa State. After World War II, Lea (then Lea Juvonen), whose family had fled from their home in Finnish Karelia when the Russians took over, came to Ames to study home economics. There she met Arne Lokken, who was studying agricultural economics. We knew them both well. After returning to Europe, they had married and here they were in Ås. Their two daughters, who spoke no English, took Kate to school each day, and the three of them skied and skated together and with other village children. The Norwegian children and our little "Finnish-Dane" evidently needed no spoken language. In Norway, most of the adults we met spoke English; many had studied in the United States.

In mid-January 1965, after our short but most pleasant stay in Norway, we left for Finland, driving the width of Sweden and ferrying from Stockholm across the ice-laden Gulf of Bothnia to Turku, where we met my cousin Aili, the daughter of my mother's sister Martha, her husband Aleksi (Alex) Uusiniemi (New Cape), and their twins, Liisa and Hannu. It was a happy moment. Aili and I were much alike both in looks and in temperament. I translated Finnish conversations for Harald and Kate and then their remarks back into Finnish for the Uusiniemis. After several hours of getting to know each other, talking, laughing, eating, we left for Helsinki with promises and plans to return to Turku another time.

In Helsinki, Antti Nikkola, whom we had known as a graduate student at the University of Minnesota, had rented us a roomy, furnished apartment. For a month, Harald would lecture and work at the Agricultural Economics Research Institute just outside Helsinki, and end with one general lecture at the University of Helsinki.

Now I had the pleasant experience of walking along the streets of Helsinki, of going into the shops and restaurants, of meeting people, and of being for the first time in a foreign country where I could understand what was spoken. However, English was generally understood and spoken in downtown Helsinki; it took a whole week before I had the courage to use only Finnish in the shops, restaurants, and post office.

Salli Pentinsaari (Benedict's Island), the daughter of my mother's sister Tyyne, came from the city of Kemi and stayed with her son, Aimo, and his wife, Pirkko-Liisa. We spent many happy hours together, and I could recognize physical characteristics and personality traits similar to our family's. Salli looked very much like my sister Irma.

Having served in the Finnish foreign service in Paris, my cousin Lassi spoke five languages—Finnish, Swedish, German, French, and English. Of all the five countries we were to visit, we felt that the Finns spoke the most languages. I surmised that they had to learn other languages because most foreigners were not about to learn Finnish, which seemed to be looked upon as a minor and very difficult language indeed.

Several times at dinner parties the conversation moved easily among three languages—Finnish, Swedish, and English. One evening's discussion centered around the discrimination against blacks as practiced in the United States, and how they in Finland viewed it. I had no pat answers. They were also intensely interested in the late President John F. Kennedy and his wife Jacqueline, whom they had revered as the "ideal" American couple. Even yet, in January, 1965, the shock of the President's assassination in 1963 was affecting them.

One morning Salli, Aili, and I took a bus to Eräjärvi (Lake in the Wilderness), my mother's childhood country home, two hours away. Here we met Elli Järvinen, my mother's half-sister, Martti Helander, her half-brother, and their families. Elli was sixty years old, Martti fifty-six. My mother was almost eighty at this time. I saw the two-room log cottage that had been Lempi's childhood home. It was still a humble home. The oldest building on the family land was an *aitta,* a small, log storage building erected in 1775. It was in this building that the bodies of my mother's baby sisters were wrapped and stored until the spring thaw made it possible for them to be buried.

My cousin Jaakko was a pipefitter and his wife Ulla worked in a creamery. On a wood-burning stove in the kitchen, Ulla cooked us

146

a fine meal. We sat at a small cloth-covered table in the center of the living room and the rest of the family sat around us but did not eat, which made us feel uncomfortable and embarrassed, especially as the children hungrily eyed the food.

On another trip, Salli, Kate, and I took a bus to the city of Lahti (Bay), north of Helsinki where Salli's youngest daughter, Irene Mäkelä, and her family lived. The one-hour trip was pleasant, with a uniformed stewardess at the bus door handling the tickets, passing out magazines once the bus was moving, and selling and serving carbonated beverages from a cooler at the front of the bus. Once again, Kate was happy to play with children even if they spoke no common language. Kate seemed proud that I could manage the language, especially on the bus. She evidently felt, and rightly so, that I hadn't done so well in Denmark or Norway. In fact, she had served as my interpreter in Sweden, using the Danish language skills she had learned in the first grade in Copenhagen.

Taking a sauna in Finland is usually a social event; one seldom bathes alone. My cousin, Helvi, her daughter Pirjo, and I were to sauna together one evening. As it happened, Pirjo decided not to come, which relieved me considerably, for after years of solitary bathing in a bathtub or shower, I was not looking forward to a group sauna. I soon discovered one of the reasons for group bathing: You wash each other's backs, which Helvi and I did after first enjoying the steam as we sat chatting on the top row of the wooden tiers, the sweat running in streams down our bodies. I must admit it was a relaxing hour we spent taking steam, slapping our bodies with birch switches, chatting, washing up, and finally returning to the dressing room to cool off. After the men enjoyed their saunas, we all sat around the kitchen table drinking coffee and eating *pulla* (cardamom coffee bread), tired but completely relaxed.

The next morning Helvi, Paavo, and I headed north toward Varpaisjärvi, my father's home village. Helvi took some days off from her teaching to join us on this trip. She now became my "mentor" and explained to me who everybody was as I was to meet many Väänänen relatives in a matter of a few days. For one week, I did not speak a word of English. This proved quite a strain on my command of Finnish, but fortunately I had with me my mother's small 1904 dictionary, *Dr. K.V. Arminen's English and Finnish Dictionary*. My copy was the third edition, published in 1914 by the Finnish Lutheran Book Concern of Hancock, Michigan.

After some hours of slippery riding on ice-covered blacktop roads, we stopped near the country village of Varpaisjärvi, at a farm called *Pinnunmäki* (Land on a Hill) at the home of our cousin Toini Ruotsalainen, whose father was our Uncle Heikki, my father's brother, whose passport my father had used. *Ruotsalainen* means a Swede. Toini's husband, Pentti, had died six years before, leaving her with six children, four of them now grown. All of them were home. The farmhouse was a lovely place, with large and airy rooms. In the *sali*, or parlor, I noted a spinning wheel, an old wooden hand-churn, colorful wall hangings, scenic paintings, bright hand-loomed rugs, and comfortable old rocking chairs.

Our next stop was Juurikkaniemi (The Cape with Stumps), one of the five farms my grandfather Heikki had worked for in order to bequeath each of his sons a farm. A pleasant surprise awaited us here. Uncle Paavo, my father's youngest brother, had driven over with Cousin Inkeri and her husband, Toivo Korolainen. Uncle Paavo was a sweet, white-haired, white-moustached seventy-six-year-old gentlemen with twinkling blue eyes. He cried when he embraced me, and I wept too. To think that it had taken over sixty years for one of his brother Otto's children to visit Otto's native land!

As we sat at the dining room table getting acquainted, eating, talking, and laughing, I noticed through a window a woman going in and out of the barn. I was told that she was the farm's *navettanainen*, or barn lady, whose main responsibility was to take care of and to milk the cows. I learned that these "barn ladies" were fairly common on Finland's large farms. The best American equivalent word would be "dairymaid."

I learned that it was customary for farm women in Finland to do much of the work on the farm. At a large farm we visited outside Helsinki, the entire dairy barn operation was run by two women. When we went into that barn, the two women, dressed in white uniforms, were operating the electric milking machines. Their husbands were hired men on the farm, and the women had trained as dairymaids. Each couple was provided a house on the farm.

Visiting another relative, we were enjoying our coffee in the afternoon when a young woman entered, helped herself to coffee at the stove, and retreated to sit on a bench beside the big oven. Rather hesitantly, I asked who she was as she had not been introduced, nor had her entrance and presence been acknowledged by the family. She was their *navettanainen*, their barn lady, or dairymaid. I got the impression that she was looked upon as their servant, one who did not eat her meals with the family, and probably lived in one of the other farm buildings, not in the farmhouse itself.

Only an old log haybarn seen across a snow-covered field remained from my father's time. With the setting sun as a backdrop, I managed to snap a picture of this aged, snow-covered haybarn, and whenever I throw this slide on the screen, I am moved with nostalgia for my father's boyhood days so long ago, so far away, so unknown to me.

One morning, we visited Kiiskimaki (Perch Hill), the farm home of my aunt, Hilma Korolainen, my father's sister and also sister of Uncle Paavo, born in 1885 and soon to celebrate her eightieth birthday. She greeted us warmly, a small, gray-haired, friendly little woman wearing a house dress and apron, both of which had seen better and cleaner days.

Our pace had been a fast one, traveling in several days to all these farms, meeting all these Väänänen relatives, sixty-eight of them. Without my cousin Helvi's help, I would have been quite confused. We did not spend much time exploring farms, for the snow was deep, the air bitter cold. I decided that one should go to Finland in summer.

I returned to Stockholm's Arlanda Airport, where Harald and Kate were waiting. During the air trip, while the stewards and stewardesses were busy selling tax-free chocolates, perfumes, liquors, and cigarettes, as we soared over the ice- and snow-covered Baltic Sea, I had the opportunity to reflect, at least a little, on my journey to my father's childhood home, its environs, its people. First of all, the countryside with its stately evergreens, its white birches, and the deep clean snow, was not a strange one, for it was much like the northern Minnesota of my childhood. The warmth and friendliness of my relatives, their reaching out to me, the joy and laughter we shared together, as if we had known each other all our lives, warmed and moved me. The years of separation from the time of my father's departure had simply seemed to dissolve and disappear. I was in tune with my Finnish relatives. I was impressed by their strength, their vitality, their good humor, their honesty. I realized that they had a sense of "place." They knew where they belonged and they were satisfied to be where they were. I did not, or I could not, tell them of my search for a place in the American mainstream, my need to hide my Finnishness, of even being ashamed of the

149

Väänänen family name, of being happy that I was known by the Scandinavian Ingrid, not the Finnish Inkeri. For the first time, I realized I loved the Finns of my childhood, the Kivipeltos, the Maenpääs, the Mäkis, the Porthans, Perttulan *Mummu.*

In my retrospective mood, I was saddened when I remembered that my father had never been able to return to the land of his birth, to meet his brothers and sisters once again, to see the old home place, to meet the friends of his youth. I wept at his loss and I am weeping as I write this, and my father has now been dead for almost forty years. There, on that flight from Finland to Sweden, I was beginning to realize that this wintry trip back into Finland was the beginning of my understanding of my own identity. I was forty-nine years old.

In April we left Sweden for Germany, for Goettingen, where for a month Harald lectured and also studied the research and teaching in agricultural economics at the University of Goettingen.

We lived in Hoffman's Hof, a guest house and farm outside the city, where no one spoke English. Harald and I managed with our college German, and later Kate told us that Fraulein Hoffman, who managed the guest house, would speak to her in English when no one else was around. She was too shy to try her English with adult Americans, but ventured it with a child.

We had come down from still wintry Sweden, looking forward to April's sun and warmth as we moved south. However, we encountered only cold and rain. To make matters worse, the heat had been turned off in the Hof. No hot water was available for baths, but there was a hot water faucet in the sink in our room, and the small room where we ate breakfast was heated for a while each morning. On some days, if Kate and I were not taking the bus into the city, we would crawl back into bed and read, staying warm and cozy under soft, down comforters, common in Europe.

Our sons spent a few days with us before returning to the United States to get summer work and to prepare for college. Harald and they went to the public baths for men, but Kate and I could never summon the courage to go to a public bath for women. We simply managed with sponge baths.

On Saturdays and Sundays, people hiked from the city to this inn to drink beer, eat sausages, potatoes, sauerkraut, dark breads, and fancy desserts—rich cakes with fruits and whipped cream. We enjoyed having the inn full of these hikers.

Our major pastime now became hiking—hiking around the old

walled city of Goettingen and in its surrounding forests. For the first time, we learned to walk for as long as six hours at a time, a truly refreshing experience.

We made many friends in the department at the University and were invited into their homes. They all spoke English. Dr. and Mrs. Arthur Hannau were old acquaintances as he had served as a visiting professor at the University of Minnesota.

The month in Germany was soon over and we set off for Belgium, for Brussels, where Harald's first Ph.D. student, Carmen Nohre, was an economist for the European Common Market. He and his family made it a pleasure to sightsee about the old city of Brussels. An unexpected pleasure was a large glass of orange juice for breakfast, something we had not had since leaving the United States.

Back in the United States

Our sons now went off to college, both with scholarships, Rudy to Carleton College in Northfield, Minnesota, and Paul to Macalester College in St. Paul. Harald, Kate, and I settled back into our old, comfortable, safe, American suburban life. Kate was in the fourth grade.

By 1968, since my homemaking duties had eased and I was seeking something more than the volunteer work I had been engaged in for a number of years, I returned to the University of Minnesota—exactly thirty years after my graduation from there. I now began to study in the field of learning disabilities. For three years (1968-1971) I worked as a tutor in a suburban junior high school, and with the help of a grant from the school district, I wrote a curriculum for the older reading-disabled student. Most of the material available at that time, as far as I could determine, was geared to the elementary student. The program I wrote sold better in states outside Minnesota than it did in Minnesota. I do not know what this means, or meant. Although the course has been out of print for a number of years, occasional orders keep coming in.

Then for a year, from August 1971 to August 1972, we lived in Arlington, Virginia, while Harald served as an economist for the State Department's Agency for International Development in Washington, D. C. We were getting a broader perspective and understanding of the United States government, and we enjoyed the standard sights of Washington, D.C., including the many art and historical museums, tours of the White House and Capitol, the Lincoln and Jefferson Memorials, sessions of Congress, the Library of Congress, Ford's Theatre, the Kennedy Center, Georgetown, Mount Vernon, Monticello, Williamsburg, and Jamestown. We were impressed by the cultural opportunities available, many of them free. Little did we realize that we would be in Washington during the break-in at the Watergate on June 17th! Most of our neighbors were employed, as Harald was, by the United States government, either in the military branch or the General Services Administration. Our immediate neighborhood was in a constant state of flux—families transferred in, transferred out. Here today but perhaps gone tomorrow, nobody seemed interested in new neighbors, but we did become well-acquainted with three families.

Our daughter Kate was now in the ninth grade. Our son Paul had entered the Ph.D. program at the Johns Hopkins School for Advanced International Studies (SAIS) at Washington, and he also worked as a truck driver for a firm selling pipe insulation, learning his way around the metropolitan area, wearing a hard hat, and hauling heavy boxes and bags of insulation to construction sites, including the White House. The owner of the insulation firm was a fellow rugby player on the SAIS team!

A Spiritual Revival with Finnish Literature

In 1973 I returned to the University of Minnesota to continue my studies in learning disabilities, after doing occasional substitute tutoring in nearby suburban schools. Knowing that I had become discouraged with the classes I was taking, our son Rudy suggested that I enroll in the Finnish program in the Department of Scandinavian Studies, in which he was enrolled as a graduate student specializing in Danish and Danish literature. So I began to audit, without credit, a class in the *Kalevala* (The District of Kaleva, or The Land of Heroes, as it is commonly known), the long narrative poem of Finland first published in 1835 after Dr. Elias Lönnrot compiled this epic poem from ancient Finnish folk poems and songs. Entering the class as an auditor I was, you see, protecting myself against failure. If the course proved too frightening, too difficult, or too uninteresting, I could drop out and just disappear from the class. However, taking this class was to make a change in the direction of my life, just as taking the teaching job at Askov, Minnesota in 1938 had changed the course of my life.

The teacher was a young woman, Hannele Jönsson, from Pori, Finland, a graduate student at the University of Helsinki. She was a diligent, capable instructor and for the first time I began to learn something about Finnish literature, that is, literature written in Finland. Most of my reading in Finnish had been Sunday School material published by the Finnish immigrant press: the *ABC Book, Luther's Catechism, Bible History.* Any other Finnish reading had seemed too difficult, even the immigrant newspapers, annuals, and magazines we subscribed to at home. A number of Finnish immigrants were writing books of fiction, plays, poetry, pamphlets, articles, but I was completely unaware of this literary output. Besides, we had learned that speaking and writing Finnish was so unAmerican, so foreign, and of what value were these skills anyway? At least no one I knew in the American "mainstream" seemed to place any value on these kinds of foreign language skills, the language skills of immigrant children.

I had, of course, heard about Elias Lönnrot and the *Kalevala* most of my life, had even attempted to read it at one time, but with little success. My knowledge of Finland's literature was just about non-existent. Now, for the first time, I learned that for many years, traveling on foot, Dr. Lönnrot had collected these ancient Finnish folk poems, had listened to Finnish and Karelian folk singers sing these old songs that had been composed orally and had been passed down through many generations by word of mouth. In 1849 the second, and more complete, edition of the *Kalevala* had appeared. Lönnrot's composing of the *Kalevala,* from his first drafts begun in 1833 until this second edition appeared in 1849, had taken sixteen years. It laid the foundation for Finnish literature. Much of written Finnish had thus far been religious-oriented, involving sermons, hymns, prayers, work of the clergy.

Now from the *Kalevala* I was to learn about Väinämöinen, the country's oldest and wisest minstrel; about Ilmarinen, the strong and dependable smith; about the boastful rogue Lemminkäinen; about the upstart singer, Joukahainen; about the tragic Kullervo. Our text was the 1963 Harvard University Press translation of Francis Peabody Magoun, Jr., English professor emeritus at Harvard.

The statement that what the immigrants' child wanted to forget, the grandchild wants to remember seemed to be proved in this class. Most of the students were undergraduates and were the grandchildren of Finnish immigrants. At fifty-eight I was the oldest student and the only immigrants' child.

One day a student, Joyce Davis, played the *kantele,* the ancient stringed instrument of the Finns, whose origin from the bones of a pike is vividly pictured in the *Kalevala,* where it was called a fishbone harp. Joyce's *kantele* had belonged to her grandfather, John Huhtala of Bovey, Minnesota, who had come to the United States at the age of nineteen. Joyce told me that as a child, she watched her grandfather play the *kantele,* and even today, mystical, romantic memories of his early playing remain with her. In her child mind, the *kantele* seemed an enormous instrument. When her grandfather was in his late seventies, she gathered the courage to ask him if he would bequeath his *kantele* to her. He was very pleased at her request, but when she asked him to teach her how to play it, he would teach her only one chord. His fingers had stiffened with age, and he could not play the *kantele* as well as he had in previous years. He did not wish to demean his earlier playing by playing poorly now. In order to leave Joyce an instrument she could be proud of, he sent to Finland for new strings. Through the years, Joyce taught herself to play and has given a number of *kantele* performances, including some at the annual Folklife Festival in 1980 at the Smithsonian Institution in Washington, D.C. In 1983 Joyce graduated from the University of Minnesota's College of Veterinary Medicine and "took back" her maiden name, Hakala. Shortly after graduation, she traveled to Finland, learning more about the *kantele*, buying a small five-stringed one, and ordering a large one with twenty-seven strings. Joyce has continued to play before many audiences and conducts a class in *kantele* playing. She and her students appear at many functions and are named *Koivun Kaiku* (Echoes Through the Birch), for the second *kantele* in the *Kalevala* was carved from a birch, which wept at such a fate.

In 1974 I registered as a bona fide but part-time student in Finnish language and literature and signed up for one class, third year Finnish, a study of Finnish prose and poetry. I had no idea how I would use this training except to satisfy some undefined yearning within me and also to assuage some feelings of guilt about being ashamed of being Finnish, feelings I had carried as a burden for a long time.

By now Rudy had finished his master's degree and his wife, Helen, was putting the finishing touches on her master's thesis, and they had left for Madison, Wisconsin, to study for their Ph.D.'s: Helen was a research assistant and Rudy a full-time student with a scholarship. Paul and his wife, Carolyn, were working and settled in Washington. Kate was a senior in high school. Harald was busy with his University work, and I had just found a new field of endeavor; what it would develop into, if anything, I had no idea.

Hannele was the teacher for this third year Finnish class, having come back from a summer in which she finished her master's degree at the University of Helsinki.

I now began to realize that I had stepped into something for which I was wholly unprepared; the reading and writing of literary Finnish on a relatively advanced level. Having spoken some Finnish daily through my first nineteen years and having written in Finnish to my parents for almost forty years, I had, in my ignorance, assumed that third year Finnish, the most advanced Finnish language level taught at the University, was where I belonged. I soon learned otherwise, and I now began a mighty struggle to unlearn my

American-style Finnish, or at least to recognize it for what it was. I needed to increase as rapidly as possible my command of a literary Finnish vocabulary, and to understand that many of the Finnish words I spoke and wrote were no longer used in Finland, for they had disappeared from the language, and were, in fact, already archaic. My parents had left Finland during the early 1900s, and it was Finnish of that vintage that we spoke at home. Hannele was also to point out that many of my words she considered dialect and colloquial. This I had not known; with our mother coming from the western province of Häme and our father from the eastern province of Savo, we children no doubt absorbed both of their dialects and colloquialisms. In addition, I came to realize that I had only a perfunctory and most elementary acquaintance with Finnish grammar as it appears in written work. Although I may have spoken relatively acceptable Finnish when dealing with simple thoughts and simple sentences with old-time immigrant Finns, I was woefully lacking in my understanding and use of grammar rules, particularly in writing.

The first assignment in the class was to read three modern short stories, each by a different author. I was discouraged, actually distraught, to find the first story filled with words completely unrecognized by me. In the first reading, I didn't understand the story at all. As a result, I read each of these three stories three times, madly devouring the Finnish dictionary during the second and third readings, before I could understand what was written.

All of my language discrepancies became readily apparent in my written answers to Hannele's questions on these three stories. My use of dialect and colloquialisms, my misuse of words, my coining of word forms that didn't even exist, my weak vocabulary, my lack of understanding of Finnish grammar, all were glaringly apparent in my writings. Somehow I had managed to stay away from American-type Finnish words, "Finnicized" English, or "Finglish," as it is usually referred to, and which was so commonly used by Finnish immigrants and their children in adapting to American culture. Today, as I look over my first papers written in that class, I do not understand why I did not just give up in despair. I was utterly discouraged and demoralized. However, through her positive criticism and her recognition of my consistently adequate understanding of the contents of the readings, Hannele did not destroy my confidence, which had been so badly shaken.

The second assignment was the reading of a modern novel, one with humorous overtones, *Pikku Pietarin Piha* (Little Peter's Courtyard) by Aapeli (Abel), the pseudonym of Simo Puupponen. This would be the first Finnish book I had ever read in its entirety. As children, we never completed the *Aapinen*, the *Catechism*, or the *Bible History* in Sunday School. During the first reading of *Little Peter's Courtyard*, I understood perhaps one-fourth of the book. After the second reading with the use of a dictionary, I could begin to write answers to Hannele's questions. During this answering process, I read most of the book a third time. The class met for an hour three times a week; I was to spend about forty hours each week in preparation for these three meetings. During the quarter, we read five more novels, a book of poetry, a play, a newspaper article. I wrote about all of these in considerable detail, working hard to develop my thought processes and writing skills in the Finnish literary language. At first, with great energy, I typed all my writing, but soon gave it up as too time consuming; the Finnish language uses a tremendous number of *ä's, ää's, ö's* and *öö's*, which took too much time to type on my typewriter, which had only ordinary keys.

And so the quarter passed, with my getting acquainted with the work of some of Finland's best writers, some of whom were: Maria Jotuni, who often wrote about women who, in dialogue form, speak of love and death; Antti Hyry, an engineer turned writer; Eeva Joenpelto, one of Finland's most successful novelists; Tove Jansson, a Finland-Swedish writer of charming fantasy tales; P. Mustapää, a classical poet, the alter ego of Professor Martti Haavio, a renowned folklore scholar; Toivo Pekkanen, a factory worker who wrote stories about the working class well enough to be elected to the prestigious and scholarly Finnish Academy; Eeva-Liisa Manner, a poet, and writer of sophisticated plays. For the first time in my life, learning was a struggle; I was trying to do something beyond my capabilities. In retrospect, I realize that I should have registered for second year Finnish, perhaps even first, before tackling the third year. From the very beginning of the course, I had begun to sign my papers not Ingrid Jensen but with my old, original Finnish name, Inkeri Väänänen. I couldn't explain why, it just seemed right.

Fortunately, the quarter that just passed turned out to be the most difficult for me. The second quarter, called "Introduction to Finnish Literature: Early Beginnings to 1900," turned out to be a chronological history of Finnish literature. Three other students had enrolled: Timo Riipa, Pirkko Hill Gaultney, and Jussi (John) Rannikko, so I was no longer alone. We were all native Finnish speakers; that is, our first spoken language had been Finnish. Two had been born in Finland, two were children of immigrants, whose first language had been Finnish.

We studied the folklore of Finland, some of it over a thousand years old, some of the themes even older. From this we moved to the work of Mikael Agricola, who pioneered and published in 1542 the first book written in the Finnish language, the *ABC-Kiria* (ABC Book). The official language of Finland had been Swedish since 1155, but at least eighty percent of the people of Finland spoke only Finnish. After Agricola's breakthrough, for many years most work written in Finnish was religious-oriented since the clergy were the educated members of Finnish society. However, by 1800 several dictionaries, newspapers, histories, and poetry written in Finnish had appeared. In 1809, through war, Finland became a grand duchy of Russia. By now the Finns knew they were not Swedes, and they certainly couldn't become Russians, so they had better just be what they really were, Finns. Publication of the *Kalevala* inspired the belief that the Finns could claim a place among civilized peoples. Their old, oral folklore showed they possessed a creative instinct. And now they had a written literature to prove it. The seeds for a national awakening had been sowed.

In the class we read some parts of the *Kalevala* in Finnish, becoming familiar with the *Kalevala* meter, trochaic tetrameter. The trochee, a poetry foot, consists of two syllables, with the accent on the first syllable. Four of these trochees, or feet, made up the *Kalevala* meter. The trochee comes naturally to the Finnish language since the first syllable in Finnish words is always accented. The American poet, Henry Wadsworth Longfellow, who had read a German translation of the Finnish *Kalevala,* used this same meter and some of the *Kalevala* themes in his *The Song of Hiawatha*, published in 1855. The *Kalevala* poems are made up of rhyming couplets, with the second line repeating the idea of the first line but in different words. Alliteration, which also comes easily to the Finnish language, plays a predominant role in all of the poems.

In 1976 I earned a bachelor's degree in Finnish language and literature. I eventually became a translator, working primarily with Finnish short stories, folk tales, and proverbs.

inna Canth, Heroine
(1844-1897)

As a student in a teachers' seminary,
She married the science professor.
Putting aside her own "idealistic pursuits"
As she called them,
She now began the tasks
Which went against her nature:
Keeping house,
Preparing meals,
Doing needlework,
Taking care of her husband,
Being an obedient wife,
Never expressing her own opinions,
For her husband's will was law in all things.
She said, "I was looked upon as a nobody."

But then one day
She dared to express her own opinions.
Surprised, her husband learned to accept them,
For she was usually proved to be right.
And he developed an unshakeable faith
In her good judgment.
As a result,
She began to write
About women's rights.
But it was too soon,
and nobody listened.
It was 1875—in Finland.

Her soul became distressed.
"Women are too feminine, too patient,
Too docile, too forbearing, too soft-hearted.
In a way, too Christian."

"Nordic women," she also wrote,
"Are quiet, faithful, meek,
Patient, obedient servants
To their husbands and children,
Not because they consider it their duty,
But simply because
They're cowards and are confused.
The issue of women's rights
Is not only one of women's rights,
But of human rights as well."

With reformist zeal
She continued to write
Articles, short stories,
And successful plays
About the limits placed on women
By society, by law, by custom,
And by religion.
She wrote about the condition of the poor.
She had the courage to criticize the Church.
Even though she herself was a religious woman,
She was branded an atheist and a free thinker.
She was called "the warlike lady of Kuopio"
And "the Amazon of freedom."
"Criticism and abuse rained on me like hail!
I lost a large number of friends,
Parents forbade their children to visit me.
But it does not matter
If one is compelled to stand alone
And to be stoned."
She kept on writing.
"Life cannot come to a halt.
It must keep moving ahead freely.
Old truths must give way
To new ones."

More remarkable does she seem
When, as a young widow,
Left with seven children,
"With nobody I could turn to,
I was sick and wretched
With no idea of how
To support my large family.
I tottered on the brink of madness."

But she took over
Her father's bankrupt fabric shop
And made of it a success.
Though often ill,
She managed the shop,
Raised her children,
And kept on writing
To become not only
The voice for women's rights,
A champion of the poor,
And a critic of the Church,
But also one of Finland's
Outstanding playwrights.

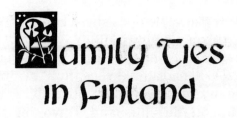

Family Ties in Finland

In the summer of 1977, my sister Irma, brother Jorma, and I flew to Finland. Irma and her family had visited Finland in 1967, two years after my first visit. Our sister Betty and her husband Wilfred, who were living in Seattle, had been to Finland in 1966. So now with Jorma making his first trip, all of the four children of Lempi Helander and Otto Väänänen would visit the land the two of them had left in their youth and to which they would never return except in memory.

By 1977, trips to Finland had become quite common for American Finns, for the aging immigrants themselves, and for their children and grandchildren. Through the cooperation of *Suomi Seura* (The Finland Society) in Finland and its offices in the United States and Canada, with the many Finnish-American organizations existing in both countries, reasonably priced trips were organized. In Minnesota the embarking point for us was Duluth, an easy trip from the Twin Cities of Minneapolis and St. Paul.

Irma and I had many joyous reunions with relatives, and they all were happy that Jorma had now also come to the land of his ancestors, the land where most of our relatives still lived.

On our mother's side of the family, most of our first cousins had died since my first trip twelve years before, but we were able to visit with our one remaining half-uncle, Martti Helander, and his wife Martta. Martti had retired from his tailoring work in the city, and the two of them had moved from the old, two-room family log house, where my mother had spent her childhood, and where I had once visited them, to an attractive house in the country not far from the village of Eräjärvi. Retired, they seemed to be happier and in better financial circumstances than when they had worked at their tailoring trade. We made a brief stop at the old home place at Eräjärvi, but our half-aunt, Elli, and her husband had both died. We were able, however, to visit our oldest cousin, Salli Pentinsaari, in her daugher's home in the city of Heinola. Salli was now seventy-seven; twelve years earlier she and I had become good friends and traveling companions in Helsinki.

On the Väänänen side of the family, Uncle Paavo had died in 1965 shortly after my first visit. His sister, our Aunt Hilma, had died in 1966—Betty and Will had attended her funeral. But Uncle Paavo's wife, Aunt Lyydiä, was still very much alive, living with her daughters, Eini and Aili, and Aili's husband, Toivo, on their home farm, Väänälä at Koukunjoki. We were able to enjoy many chats with her; she was now almost eighty. Cousin Paavo, my chauffeur in 1965, was married now, had two sons, worked and lived in Helsinki.

Koulu Inkeri's husband, Väinö, had died of cancer. The old country school where Inkeri had taught had closed, and she taught now in the city of Iisalmi and lived there in a comfortable apartment, where she entertained us.

We also visited our cousin, Helvi Vaisanen, in Pieksämäki. Their five children had left home and she and her husband, Matti, had sold their large house, where I had visited them, and they now lived in a light, airy apartment. Helvi and her best friend, Hilja Hokkanen, had visited us in the United States in 1975, and we were treated royally by Hilja when we visited her in the city of Joensuu.

Some of our most delightful days in Finland were spent with our cousin Lassi Väänänen, Uncle Paavo's youngest son, his wife Sinikka, and their four children at their large summer home at Otalampi (Point on the Lake), twenty kilometers from Helsinki. Here we enjoyed many saunas followed by refreshing swims in the clear, cool water; we rowed about the lake in their graceful yellow and blue rowboat; we played tennis on their court among the pines, and badminton on a small court beside their cottage. At midnight, when it was still light, we often roasted fish and *makkaroita* (sausages) over an open fire on a hill above the shore. The family moved here for the summer, with Lassi and Sinikka driving each day to Helsinki to work—Lassi as an engineer in wood products and Sinikka as the owner-manager of her family's decorating studio and store. Sinikka's sister, Anneli, married to a judge in Spain, was spending the summer at Otalampi with her three Spanish-speaking children, who were quickly learning to speak Finnish. Also at the cottage was Sinikka and Anneli's mother, Saima Kemppäinen, who had suffered a series of strokes and could no longer live alone in her Helsinki apartment. Thus there were twelve of us at the cottage, sometimes fourteen if the children had guests. Besides the many bedrooms in the large cottage, there were two sleeping cabins on the property, so sleeping accommodations were most adequate. This stay at Otalampi was a pleasant interlude. When we rode into Helsinki with Lassi and Sinikka on occasional mornings, we had the use of their roomy, comfortable apartment within walking distance of the city center. We entertained some of our American friends here and also left from Helsinki to visit other relatives and friends.

I was fortunate to visit in relatives' homes with good libraries as I was able to add to my growing list of short stories to translate—a project always on my mind.

It was also encouraging to discover that many of our various cousins' children were able to speak English—although most of them were too shy to attempt very much in the presence of these American relatives.

In her family's 1967 visit to Finland, my sister Irma had become acquainted with her husband's relatives, the Parssinens, uprooted Karelian refugees, some of whom were now successful farmers in Finland, some successful businessmen, others now retired. They were lively, gay, full of life and conversation, as Karelians are reputed to be. It was a satisfying experience to meet one extended family of Finland's "displaced" people and to observe how well they had adapted to their lives in Finland after fleeing from Karelia and its Russian occupation.

It was a great pleasure to visit once again in Finland, and I fleetingly entertained the idea that I would like to live for at least one summer on Aunt Lyydiä's farm, to talk with our many relatives, to spend time on the river, to read, to write. But of course, home responsibilities called us back to the United States.

Some Thoughts about the Finnish Language

During my growing-up years, our neighbors and casual acquaintances were of many nationalities, few of them "American," which I defined as English-speaking, white, Anglo-Saxon, Protestant. Most of my friends were children of immigrants—Polish, Italian, Slovenian, Finnish, Norwegian, Swedish. I had no "American" friends. As I remember, the Finnish accent was the most imitated and ridiculed.

A town in Michigan was named Bruce's Crossing. People laughed when the Finns pronounced it "Ruce's Rossing." But there are good reasons for this pronunciation. First of all, the letters "b" and "c" do not exist in the native Finnish language. In addition, no old, genuine Finnish words begin with more than one consonant (consonant blends or clusters), such as the "br" and "cr" in Bruce's Crossing, or such as tr, fr, pl, and sl. For most immigrant Finns it was impossible to pronounce these blends. As a result, it was "ruck" for truck, "Rans" for France (the Finnish word for France is Ranska, with no "fr" cluster), "layer" for player, "lippery" for slippery—actually often "lipri," if not "lipi." "Pretty slippery outside" came out "Puti lipi outside."

In addition to having no "b" and "c," the Finnish language does not use the letters f, q, w, x, and z, except in words of foreign origin, so these letter sounds in the English language were new to most immigrants. To further complicate matters, the letters "d" and "g" never begin Finnish words. Both of these letters appear only within a word; "t" changes to "d" according to a technique called consonant gradation. For example, katu (street) becomes kadun in its genitive form; "g" is always preceded by an "n" as in rengas (ring or tire) and in kuningas (king).

In a 1968 Finnish-English dictionary, all the words beginning with b, c, d, f, and g are loan words, borrowed from other languages, and not indigenous to the Finnish language, words usually not known to the emigrating Finn. Not a single word is listed under q, *w, x,* and *z*. If *"w"* does appear in a Finnish word, and this usually occurs in proper names, it is pronounced *v* and found with the *v*'s in the dictionary.

The five consonants—*k, p, s, t, v*—are the most common initial, or beginning, letters in Finnish words. Well over half the words in the dictionary begin with one of these letters. The only consonants that end Finnish words are *n, s, t, r,* and *l*.

Finnish is a phonetically regular language. Once learned, pronunciation of vowels, vowel combinations, and consonants remains the same; each sound remains constant. For example, the various sounds of the vowel *a* are: *a, aa, ä, ää, ai, äi, äy,* and these retain their "original" pronunciations regardless of the words in which they appear. In Finnish, the letter *y* is always a vowel, with only one pronunciation; in English the sound of *y* differs in yes, happy, sky; here *y* is first a consonant, then a "short" vowel, and finally a "long" vowel, each pronounced differently, yet it is the same letter. I wonder how a Finn first pronounced eye!

Another example giving trouble to the Finns was what is often called a "magic e" rule: *pan* plus *e* equals pane. Reading phonetically, a Finn would read pane with two syllables, *pa·ne*. One can imagine a Finn's consternation when confronted with *ph* as in phonograph, philosophy; with *ei* as in seize, either, neither, weird, leisure, forfeit, foreign, height, weight, neighbor, to say nothing about *ough* in ought, thought, enough, though, through, cough, trough, and hiccough, and also *augh* as in aught, caught, draught, daughter, laugh, and laughter. One writer composed the following sentence demonstrating some of these difficulties: "As I was ploughing through a rough field by the slough I saw a trough full of dough, and it gave me the hiccoughs." All of this was enough to make a phonetically oriented Finn throw up his hands in despair, to simply give up on the English language, to retreat into the safety of his own language, to choose to live in a Finnish area, which many of them did.

Another problem involved the pronouns "he" and "she." Who was a "he" and who was a "she?" Finnish has no separate feminine or masculine gender. The pronoun *hän* can be either "he" or "she" and the possessive *hänen* either "his" or "hers." When you say *Hän tuli* you do not know whether it's a "he" or a "she" who came, *tuli* meaning came. The clue to gender must be found elsewhere than in the brief remark, *"Hän tuli."* *"Se,"* the neuter "it," can refer to animals and things but also, in an informal way, to people. *"Se tuli"* can mean "The dog came," "The car came," "The man came," "The woman came." Here again the gender must be found elsewhere than in the brief remark, *"Se tuli."* Needless to say, whether to say "she," "he," or "it" in English caused the immigrant Finns a lot of embarrassment.

We city Finn kids, exposed daily outside the home to much spoken English, learned quickly to speak American "English" with little or no accent, or so we thought. But many Finnish farm children spoke with a heavy Finnish accent. Living on isolated farms, the parents, particularly the mothers, had little opportunity to learn or even to hear English, so only Finnish was usually spoken to the parents, especially to the mother.

The country stores were usually run by Finns, most of the neighboring farmers were Finnish, and Finnish was the language used in the churches and societies in the rural communities as well, of course, as in the city churches and societies. The Finnish accent was particularly noticeable to us when rural Finnish children, before the county high schools were established in the rural districts, came to the ninth grade in Junior High School. Some could not adjust to life in the city school and soon dropped out.

Since we Finnish kids learned our English in the public schools and not at home, our English generally was grammatically correct. We were not learning the "broken English" of our parents. In speaking to our parents, we always called them *"Isä"* (Father) and *"Äiti"* (Mother). For some reason we could never call them "Mom and Dad" or "Mama and Papa." These were too American! When we spoke to others about our parents we always said "my mother" and "my father," never "my mom" or "my dad." Somehow these terms just did not come naturally to us. In speaking in English to each other about our parents, we children called them simply "Ma" and "Pa."

Students learning the Finnish language complain about the impossible length of the words. For example: *sairaalatarvikkeet,* (hospital supplies), *hallintoviranoimainen* (executive), *vaikealaatuisuus* (seriousness), *valehteliminen* (lying). Often a long Finnish word will represent several English words. For instance, *muinaissuomalaisillakin* means "even among the ancient Finns." *Kansanvälinentyöleirijärjestö* means "international work camp organization." The longest word I could find has thirty-four (count them) letters: *tilliliemessäkeitetty-kalakääryleet.* It means "sole in dill sauce," but what the Finns are actually saying is "fish rolls baked in a dill sauce." In addition, the Finnish language has the distinction of having the longest known palindromic word, a word that has the same spelling both forward and backward. It is the nineteen-letter word, *saippuakivikauppias,* meaning a dealer in lye.

Finnish is also a language in which a whole poem can be made using only two letters, *k* and *o,* buttressed with two *n's:*

"Kokoo kokoon koko kokko."
"Koko kokkoko kokoon?"
"Koko kokko!"

Roughly translated, it means:

"Put the whole bonfire together."
"The whole bonfire together?"
"The whole bonfire!"

American Finns had a word they used when everything was going well, when everything was just rosy. It was *kukkelikuu,* a bright and cheerful word for a Finn to say or to hear. Another phrase, used by Finns and others, even by non-Finnish kids on the street, was *"Haista napa!"* Its meaning is similar to "Oh, go fly a kite," but the exact translation is "Smell your bellybutton!" An American expletive popular also among the Finns was "Oh, sit!" The *sh* sound was a difficult one for the Finns.

Once we learned English, we immigrant children chortled with glee over some of the language errors the Finns made, and on occasion we had fun with our Americanized Finnish. We used to laugh about the following sentence, in which every word is Americanized Finnish: *"Pussaa peipipokia kitsistä petiruumaan,"* which means "Push the baby buggy from the kitchen into the bedroom." In Finland Finnish, the sentence reads, *"Vie vauvan vaunu keittiöstä sänkykamariin,"* a statement completely foreign to us American Finn kids.

I have a recipe written by my mother, which is an example of some of the problems confronting a phonetically oriented writer from Finland:

3   kuppia crehamkrakes
1   kup Evanpurodet milk
1   kup saklet sips
1/4 kup nats
1   kup sugar

Some Finnish language purists have sometimes accused the American Finns of corrupting the Finnish language and have ridiculed the American-type Finnish words, which constitute a "mongrel" language sometimes called "Finglish." However, it was through these very words that the immigrants and we, their children, adapted the Finnish language to life in the American society. Ninety-eight percent of the Finnish immigrants could read and write their own language, but Finland was a rural society, and no Finnish words existed for the many modern inventions and ideas the immigrants met in the United States. So it was easy to call a city alley an *äli*, a car a *kaara*, a fender a *fenteri*, a gear a *keeri*, traffic *raffikki*, a tire a *taijeri*. We children slipped easily into this American-type Finnish. Following are examples of English nouns and verbs we modified into Finnish. I am sure that readers with Finnish backgrounds can add many more from their own experience.

English	Americanized Finnish	Finnish
	Nouns	
apple	äpyli	omena
baker	paakari	leipuri
bathroom	paatiruuma	kylpyhuone
bean	pinssi	papu
birthday	pörttei	syntymäpäivä
blanket	länketti	peite, viltti
brake	rekki	jarru
bus depot	possitipo	linjavaunu asema
cabbage	käpetsi	kaali
candy	känti	makeinen
carrot	käretsi or keltajuuri	porkkana
cigaret	sikuretti	savuke
corn	koorni	maissi
engine	inssi	kone
goodbye	kupai	hyvästi
ham	hämmi	kinkku
high-toned	haituuni	hieno, upea
highway	haivei	valtatie
house	houssi	talo
job	japi	työ
kitchen	kitsi	keittiö, kyökki
lake	leeki	järvi
lawyer	loijari	lakimies
machine	masina	kone
mine	maini	kaivos

English	Americanized Finnish	Finnish
	Nouns	
miner	mainari	kaivosmies
orange	orenssi	appelsiini
porch	portsi	veranta
post office	posti offiisi	postikonttori
shovel	soveli	lapio
sidewalk	saitvooki	kavelytie
store	toori, stoori	kauppa
teacher	titseri	opettaja
telephone	telefooni	puhelin
toilet	toiletti	hyysikkä (now archaic)
trouble	ropeli	huoli

English	Americanized Finnish	Finnish
	Verbs	
to call	kaalata	kutsua, soittaa
to count	kaunttaa	merkitä
to fail	feilata	epäonnestua
to farm	farmata	viljellä
to lose	luusata	kadottaa
to mine	mainata	kaivaa
to pick	pikata	poimia
to rake	reikatta	haravoida
Shut up!	Serap!	Ole hiljaa!

In almost all of the nouns listed, "i" forms the ending for the American-Finnish words; "i" is the predominant vowel in the Finnish language. We used to laugh and say, "To make a Finnish word out of an American word, just end it with an "i."

Many of us had never heard the Finnish words for which we were substituting the American-Finnish ones. We never knew, for instance, that a carrot was called a *porkkana*. We simply called it a *käretsi* or *keltajuuri*, a yellow root. Since beet in Finnish is a *punajuuri*, a red root, we just assumed a carrot was a yellow root. We never knew that an orange was an *appelsiini*, at least not until we were grown. We just used *orenssi*.

Some words we translated directly from English into American Finnish. Ice cream became *jää kermaa* while the Finland-Finnish term is *jäätelo*. Airplane became *ilmalaiva*, meaning airship, while the Finnish term is *lentokone*, a flying machine. Since we knew no Finnish equivalent for plane, we simply used ship, but this was a great mistake as an airship is a dirigible, as the Finland Finns knew so well. To compound the offense, we called the airport an *ilmalaiva kenttä*, an airship field, when it was in truth a *lentokenttä*, a flying field. Many an American Finn suffered laughter and mild ridicule from relatives and friends when he or she made that first *ilmalaiva* trip to Finland.

Some words our family always used in the Finnish form, never making American-Finnish words from them:

English	Finnish	English	Finnish	English	Finnish
aunt	täti	father	isä	cousin	serkku
bread	leipä	girl	tyttö	sleep (*verb*)	nukkuu
brother	veli	God	Jumala	sleep (*noun*)	uni
butter	voi	home	koti	son	poika
cat	kissa	money	raha	song	aulu
church	kirkko	mother	äiti	uncle	setä
door	ovi	sister	sisko		

It is interesting to note that many of these words carry an emotional connotation: mother, father, sister, brother, son, aunt, uncle, home, church, sleep, song. It could also be that the words were more easily said in Finnish than in the American-type Finnish.

Being Finnish in America

Our parents didn't talk very much about their lives in the Old Country. Perhaps they felt we weren't interested, that we were interested in being Americans, not Finns. And so we were. We resisted their attempts to talk about Finland. We closed our ears and minds to talk about Finland. Their attachment to the Old Country became boring to us. For nowhere, except among the Finns themselves, did we in our childhood ever hear of values attached to our foreign backgrounds, not even to those of the Greek and Italian kids, whose backgrounds, however long ago, had, after all, been the glories of Greece and Rome. In school, the varied immigrant backgrounds of most of the Range students were simply ignored, if not ridiculed.

When a young St. Paul woman went to teach in Eveleth in the fall of 1908, she wrote this to her parents about Eveleth: "The children in this third grade belong to the foreign population with the exception of one child. They say there are 10,000 people here, but only about 2,000 civilized folk—of the others the Austrians and the Finns are the majority."

She also wrote the following to her parents: "Mrs. Samuelson, my landlady, is a strange creature. Her Finnish name is Mikki Koukkari. She is a rabid Socialist and all the Socialists who come here to speak stay at her house. One came Saturday night and they had a grand to-do down in the kitchen till two in the morning. Socialism is rampant here among the miners."

When I was among Finns, I was proud to be a Finn; yet, when I was among Americans, I was ashamed of being a Finn—ashamed of my Finnish name. What kind of a name was Inkeri Väänänen for an American girl? I have read that Leonard Woolf, the husband of the famous British writer, Virginia Woolf, was proud of being Jewish but also ashamed of it. He loved his family, yet he hated them, too.

As a child and even as an adult, I looked upon myself not as an American but as a Finn who lived in America. The term, Finnish-American, was not known to us. We were not Finnish-Americans,

Swedish-Americans, Polish-Americans, Italian-Americans, Croatian-Americans. We were Finns, Swedes, Poles, Italians, Croatians. We did not look upon ourselves as hyphenated Americans.

We were, most of us, immigrant laborers' children, whose parents, seeking lives better than they had in the Old Country, had come to America during the time when immigration to the United States was essentially unrestricted, unrestricted at least until the early 1920s, when immigration quota laws were passed, which effectively cut off immigration from eastern and southern Europe. But by that time many immigrants were already here.

The immigrant parents of all the nationalities I knew as a child were, for the most part, young, hard-working, family oriented, filled with a desire to succeed in this strange new land, wanting education and opportunities for their children so their children's lives would be better than theirs had been in the Old Country, better than their lives were here in this new country. These parents were willing to work at menial jobs.

Because English was such an extremely difficult language for most of them, many Finns worked for years at low level jobs in the iron mines or forests, at the sawmills or railroads, or slaved on their meager, soil-poor, cutover farms. Because of this language barrier, most of them were estranged from the culture of the American society. But their families, their friends, their churches, their halls, their many societies provided opportunities for enriching their lives. In my memory at least, it seemed that among the immigrants on the Iron Range, the Finns particularly drew much strength from all the groups they belonged to: the church congregations, the temperance societies, the cooperative societies, the Socialist Federation, the Industrial Workers of the World, the Communist groups, the church ladies' aids, the cooperative guilds, and within these organizations the many choirs and choruses, orchestras and bands, athletic teams, drama groups, poetry, and reading clubs, lending libraries, summer camps, and the numerous festivals.

In many parts of the United States, the Finns built, besides churches, hundreds of other buildings to house all these activities, halls that came to be known as Finn Halls. These all served as a second home to the Finnish immigrants. Here they could speak their own language freely, find friends, exchange ideas, listen to speeches, see plays, hear poetry read, borrow books to read, sing, dance, eat Finnish foods, and drink coffee. Sometimes these social and cultural activities seemed more important to the immigrants than the ideologies of the groups they joined. But here they found release from the pressures of the alien American world. Here they were secure among their own. None of us knew then that some day all of this would be explained away by historians and sociologists as "life in a Finnish subculture."

Somehow, we children were made aware that we were in a melting pot; that we, the children of immigrants, were expected to become Americans even if our parents could not. In the 1920s it seemed as if the language we spoke at home, our foreign customs, our family's emotional ties to the Old Country were better abandoned, that we should turn into Americans, or at least make the attempt. We immigrant children learned early that not only were we different, but also that we were inferior to the Americans. However, we were to be made into genuine members of the American society.

And we did try hard to be what Americans wanted us to be, or what in our minds we *thought* Americans wanted us to be. We knew, of course, that *real* American kids had handsome, tall, slender, well-dressed, English-speaking mothers and fathers, with no foreign accents or "broken" English, that they had easy-to-pronounce last names like Brown, Jones, Smith, Richards, Roberts, and first names like Bobby, Jack, Jimmy, Mary Jane, Phyllis, Nancy. To us, these were the *native* Americans, not the Indians in northern Minnesota, who were, to us, just another displaced group, like us. Most of our Finnish names, both first and last, were a dead giveaway about our foreign and humble origins; the majority of Finnish immigrants were unskilled rural people who had fled land-poor Finland. Our last names—Vainionpää, Pylvälä, Väyrynen, Särkipato, Hirvivaara— were unpronounceable by the American tongue. Our first names, Orvokki, Lahja, Kyllikki, Veikko, Väinö, Yrjö were also strange to the American ear.

Perhaps without being consciously aware of it, we thought of ourselves, and most certainly of our parents, as marginal people in America, not really Americans, or at least not what we perceived *real* Americans to be—white, Anglo-Saxon, English-speaking, Protestant. I felt honored when someone said, "But you don't *look* Finnish." We hated it when someone remarked, "She's got the map of Finland on her face." We wanted so to pass into the American stream—as we construed that stream.

Among the immigrant groups, the Finns had an extra burden to

175

carry. For a long time the Finns were looked upon as Mongolians on the basis of a book written as long ago as 1775 by the German anthropologist, J.F. Blumenbach, who had divided the world's people into five races, based on color of skin. Since the Finns didn't fit easily into any of the five races, he lumped them in with the Mongols. Blumenbach's work had been the basis for all subsequent racial classifications and had been passed from one reference work to another, until anthropologists finally realized that something was wrong.

The court case of the Finn, John Svan vs. the U.S. government, threatened to prevent any Finn from becoming an American citizen on the ground that Finns were Mongolians, not "white persons" within the meaning of Section 2169, United States Revised Statutes. They were ineligible for citizenship based on a series of Oriental Exclusion Acts passed in 1882, 1892, 1902. On January 4, 1908, Swan and sixteen other Finns were denied citizenship by District Attorney John C. Sweet of St. Paul. However, on January 17 of that same year, Judge William A. Cant, at the U.S. District Court, sitting in Duluth, officially declared that the Finns were not of the yellow race, that though perhaps the Finns had been "Mongols" in the remote past, their blood had so been tempered by that of the Teutonic and other races that they "are now among the whitest people in Europe." Evidently this relieved the Finns greatly, for they had adopted Western attitudes toward the yellow race. Reverberations from this controversy on Mongolianism were still in the air during my childhood. In fact, as late as 1957, the issue of Mongolianism still bothered many Finns. In that year, the Knights and Ladies of Kaleva, a middle-class fraternal group of Finns, commissioned an amateur anthropologist to write a book "scientifically" disproving, once and for all, the theory that Finns are Asians.

In a 1938 issue of the *Päivälehti*, the Finnish daily newspaper published in Duluth, Kaarina Leino-Olli wrote about her experiences as a Finnish child growing up in Ely, Minnesota:

"Why did we Finns who were growing up around 1915 feel ourselves so inferior? First of all, because we belonged to a small nationality group, which in addition to everything else had come from a country of which nobody knew anything at all or only so much, perhaps, that it was some North Russian province. If the name of Finland meant anything at all to an average American, it brought to mind images of a frozen wilderness of reindeer and of

176

Lapps peering out of their leather hoods with slanting eyes. If someone said, 'My parents were born in Finland,' he was usually asked, 'Where's that?' And although we children were born in America, we were usually called foreigners just the same. The irony of it was that those who accused us of being foreigners or worse were frequently foreigners themselves, but from England or Ireland, and since they spoke the language of the country, they considered themselves very superior, even though they often were very simple people.

"Yes, they called us foreigners, and in less charitable moments they called us bums or dirty Finns. Geography books, encyclopedias, and social studies always used to state that Finns were Mongolians. It is difficult to describe to you who have been able to avoid these labels how it froze the heart and how it could crush a child. I shall never forget what happened to me once when I was about ten years old. Near us lived an Irish family, with a daughter named Kathleen who also had a nickname, Sunny. One afternoon we had been playing together with our dolls, and when suppertime approached, I said, 'Good-bye, Sunny, I guess I have to go home now.' To my horror she replied to me angrily, 'Don't you call me Sunny. You're a dirty Finn; you must call me Kathleen.'

"I was left speechless with humiliation after this unexpected retort. I went home, bitter and depressed, wondering what really was the matter with Finns and why I had been born one.

"I remember how a Finnish girl, whose name was Sirkka, used to be teased in school. Somehow or other the rest of the children had found out that Siirka derived from *heinasirkka,* meaning grasshopper, and so that is what they sarcastically called her from that time on, grasshopper. Impi became Imp, Tyyne became Tiny, Tellervo became Telephone. You may be smiling, as I am now, at these childish cruelties, but to those children whose names were twisted about and laughed at, it was no joking matter. Some were so hurt by it that they Anglicized their names whenever possible. It must be noted that these same Finnish children growing up and becoming parents, gave their own children English names. Among their children you will not find any named Toivo, Impi, or Lempi. And considering the situation, they can hardly be blamed for it."

On the Range, where so many nationalities existed side by side, one of the first questions many of us asked when we met someone new, was "What nationality are you?" It seemed such a natural question to ask a newcomer. Later, when we lived in the state of Kentucky, I came to realize that this question had absolutely no meaning for most of the people we met there, people whose Anglo-Saxon ancestors had come to this country long ago. They simply didn't understand what the question meant. "Why, what do you mean, 'What nationality am I?' I'm an American, of course!"

Many of the various Range nationalities engaged to some degree in name calling, using offensive names to refer to each other's nationalities: Italians were Wops or Dagoes (wine was Dago red); Jews were Kikes, Sheenies, Yids; Slavs were Bohunks or Hunkies; Poles were dumb Polacks; Cornish miners, Cousin Jacks; Danes, Squareheads; Swedes were dumb Swedes; Norwegians, Herring Chokers or Norskies; Chinese were Chinks, Coolies; the Irish were Shanty Irish or Lace Curtain Irish; the black man was a Coon or a Nigger. We called Brazil nuts niggertoes, without ever realizing what we were actually saying. In our neighborhood the members of a Polish family named Ciez were simply called The Cheeses.

As Finns we were often referred to as those dumb Finlanders, those dirty Finlanders. As a result, Finlander became a deprecating, belittling term in my mind. To this day, even though I know that Finlander is an appropriate term designating inhabitants of Finland, I still bridle a little when I read it or hear it.

Two Finnish men's names, Toivo (Hope) and Urho (Hero or Champion) were frequently the names of characters in disparaging jokes about Finns—jokes which the Finns seemed to enjoy as much as anyone, but usually only if they were told by a fellow Finn. If someone not a Finn told a disparaging joke about Finns, not only did we feel he was making fun of us and we were being insulted, but we also felt as if an outsider was usurping something that really belonged to us Finns.

We felt the purpose of these jokes was to subject us to ridicule—especially when they were told by an "outsider" imitating a Finnish accent. If a child lives with ridicule, he learns to be shy and we Finnish kids, most of us, *were* shy. These jokes seemed to be a measure of how we were regarded by others; they denigrated us, they created an inferiority complex in us, and we Finns had that in full enough measure without the added pain from these jokes. We cringed and were helpless before them, and we were made even more insecure about our Finnish roots. We were not sophisticated enough to recognize that the jokes were an assault on the dignity of the human spirit. That bigotry lay just under the surface. And yet, when a Finn told a joke about Finns, perhaps even the same joke that was told by an "outsider," we could laugh and be healed.

# Mother's Fear

Somehow Mother had changed.
She now seemed gripped with fear.
Although she had good renters
In the four rooms upstairs,
She felt isolated and alone downstairs
In this house where she'd lived for fifty years.
Just before she died at eighty-nine
We finally learned the source of her fear.
Her friend and neighbor
Had been found by relatives
Beside her telephone,
. . . .Dead for three days. . . .

emembering Mother

My mother has been dead
For almost twenty years,
Yet now I think of her often—
At night just before I fall asleep,
Also in the morning when I awaken.
I think of all the things
We *should* have talked about—
About her two sisters, her one brother,
And their family life in Finland.
About the void left
After their mother's early death,
When a stepmother arrived—too soon.
About her years as a spinner
In a Swedish textile mill.
Of her expectations when, at twenty-six,
She sailed away to America,
To America, the great hope
Of millions like her,
Who sailed away to open
That golden door to that golden land.
I never asked her
Whether she was glad she had come
To live her life in a land
Where she remained forever a foreigner.
Although her children could speak her language,
American English became their favored tongue.
For many years she lived alone,
A widow for twenty-six years.
All four children had moved away.
In the end, at eighty-nine,
No family was with her
When she died
In a nursing home
In America.

he Wall Hanging

Musta tulpaani

For over fifty years it has hung on a wall,
First in the modest front room
Of our family's immigrant home,
And now on the wall of my American home.

Five large, black-edged red tulips
Burst out of a sunburned field of rust,
Their heavy green leaves
Grow out of long brown stems.

It came, a gift from my mother's sisters,
From the then faraway land of the North,
Sent across the ocean, more than fifty years ago
To the sister who had dared to cross the great sea.

Though she would live to be eighty-nine,
She would never see her homeland again,
Nor her two sisters, who remembered her so well
With letters, family pictures, this beloved wall hanging.

And so this black tulip wall hanging,
First on her wall and now on mine,
Bears witness of a link to that Old Country,
And remains one of the ties that still binds.

Inkeri Väänänen-Jensen

Addendum

I have wept often as I have written the manuscript for this book, and I have wept also during the nights as I have thought of the many Finnish immigrants of my childhood, including my parents, whose lives have ended, yet who still remain alive in my memory.

About the Author

Inkeri Väänänen-Jensen, daughter of Finnish immigrants, has earned degrees in English and in Finnish from the University of Minnesota. In 1973 she began the study of Finnish language, literature, and history. She wrote one chapter of the book *Sampo, the Magic Mill*, edited by Aili Jarvenpa and Michael Karni, published by New Rivers Press, Minneapolis, and also for the book *In Two Cultures*, edited by Jarvenpa. Väänänen-Jensen has translated four books from Finnish to English—*Finnish Short stories, Finnish Proverbs, The Fish of Gold and Other Finnish Folk Tales*, and *Forbidden Fruit and Other Tales by Juhani Aho*, all published by Penfield Press of Iowa City, Iowa.

Inkeri's husband, Harald Jensen, retired from the University of Minnesota, serves on the board of the Danish Immigrant Museum at Elk Horn, Iowa. Their children: Rudy is a professor of Scandinavian Studies at Grand View College, Des Moines, Iowa. Paul is first vice-president and founding partner of a public affairs and public relations company in Washington, D.C. Daughter Kate is an associate professor of French and French literature at Louisiana State University, Baton Rouge.